Praise for
A LONG WAY GONE

"Beah . . . speaks in a distinctive voice, and he tells an important story."
—JOHN CORRY, *The Wall Street Journal*

"Americans tend to regard African conflicts as somewhat vague events signified by horrendous concepts—massacres, genocide, mutilation— that are best kept safely at a distance. Such a disconnect might prove impossible after reading *A Long Way Gone*, . . . a clear-eyed, undeniably compelling look at wartime violence . . . *Gone* finds its power in the revelation that under the right circumstances, people of any age can find themselves doing the most unthinkable things."
—GILBERT CRUZ, *Entertainment Weekly*

"His honesty is exacting, and a testament to the ability of children 'to outlive their sufferings, if given a chance.'" —*The New Yorker*

"This absorbing account . . . goes beyond even the best journalistic efforts in revealing the life and mind of a child abducted into the horrors of warfare . . . Told in clear, accessible language by a young writer with a gifted literary voice, this memoir seems destined to become a classic firsthand account of war and the ongoing plight of child soldiers in conflicts worldwide."
—*Publishers Weekly* (starred review)

"Deeply moving, even uplifting . . . Beah's story, with its clear-eyed reporting and literate particularity—whether he's dancing to rap, eating a coconut or running toward the burning village where his family is trapped—demands to be read."
—LIZA NELSON, *People* (Critic's Choice, four stars)

"Beah is a gifted writer . . . Read his memoir and you will be haunted . . . It's a high price to pay, but it's worth it."
—MALCOLM JONES, *Newsweek.com*

"When Beah is finally approached about the possibility of serving as a spokesperson on the issue of child soldiers, he knows exactly what he wants to tell the world . . . 'I would always tell people that I believe children have the resilience to outlive their sufferings, if given a chance.' Others may make the same assertions, but Beah has the advantage of stating them in the first person. That makes *A Long Way Gone* all the more gripping." —CAROL HUANG, *The Christian Science Monitor*

"In place of a text that has every right to be a diatribe against Sierra Leone, globalization or even himself, Beah has produced a book of such self-effacing humanity . . . *A Long Way Gone* transports us into the lives of thousands of children whose lives have been altered by war, and it does so with a genuine and disarmingly emotional force."
—RICHARD THOMPSON, *Star Tribune* (Minneapolis)

"It would have been enough if Ishmael Beah had merely survived the horrors described in *A Long Way Gone*. That he has written this unforgettable firsthand account of his odyssey is harder still to grasp. Those seeking to understand the human consequences of war, its brutal and brutalizing costs, would be wise to reflect on Ishmael Beah's story." —CHUCK LEDDY, *The Philadelphia Inquirer*

"Beah's memoir is off the charts in its harrowing depictions of cruelty and depravity. What saves it from being a gratuitous immersion in violence is his brilliant writing, his compelling narrator's voice, his gift for telling detail . . . This war memoir haunts the heart long after the eyes have finished the final page."
—JOHN MARSHALL, *Seattle Post-Intelligencer*

ISHMAEL BEAH

A LONG
WAY GONE

Ishmael Beah was born in Sierra Leone in 1980. He moved to the United States in 1998 and finished his last two years of high school at the United Nations International School in New York. He graduated from Oberlin College in 2004. He is a member of the Human Rights Watch Children's Rights Division Advisory Committee and has spoken before the United Nations, the Council on Foreign Relations, the Center for Emerging Threats and Opportunities (CETO) at the Marine Corps Warfighting Laboratory, and many other NGO panels on children affected by war. He is also the head of the Ishmael Beah Foundation, which is dedicated to helping former child soldiers reintegrate into society and improve their lives. His work has appeared in *VesperinePress* and *LIT* magazine. He lives in Brooklyn.

A LONG
WAY GONE

Memoirs of a Boy Soldier

❦

ISHMAEL BEAH

SARAH CRICHTON BOOKS
Farrar, Straus and Giroux
New York

SARAH CRICHTON BOOKS
Farrar, Straus and Giroux
18 West 18th Street, New York 10011

Grateful acknowledgment is made for permission to reprint excerpts from the
following previously published material:
"O.P.P.," words and music by Vincent Brown, Keir Gist, and Anthony Criss
(interpolates elements of "ABC," by Deke Richards, Frederick Perren, Alphonso Mizell,
and Berry Gordy, Jr.), copyright © 1991 by WB Music Corp., Naughty Music, and
Jobette Music, Inc. All rights on behalf of itself and Naughty Music administered by
WB Music Corp. All rights reserved. Used by permission of Alfred Publishing Co., Inc.

The Library of Congress has cataloged the hardcover edition as follows:
Beah, Ishmael, 1980–
    A long way gone : memoirs of a boy soldier / by Ishmael Beah. —1st ed.
        p. cm.
    "Sarah Crichton Books."
    ISBN-13: 978-0-374-10523-5 (hardcover : alk. paper)
    ISBN-10: 0-374-10523-5 (hardcover : alk. paper)
    1. Beah, Ishmael, 1980–   2. Sierra Leone—History—Civil War,
1991—Personal narratives.   3. Sierra Leone—History—Civil War,
1991—Participation, Juvenile—Biography.   4. Child soldiers—Sierra
Leone—Biography.   5. Sierra Leone—Social conditions—1961–
1. Title.

DT516.828.B43 A3 2007
966.404—dc22
[B]

2006017101

Paperback ISBN-13: 978-0-374-53126-3
Paperback ISBN-10: 0-374-53126-9

Designed by Cassandra J. Pappas

www.fsgbooks.com

30 29 28 27 26 25 24 23

To the memories of
Nya Nje, Nya Keke,
Nya Ndig-ge sia, and Kaynya.
Your spirits and presence within me
give me strength to carry on,

to all the children of Sierra Leone
who were robbed of their childhoods,

and

to the memory of Walter (Wally) Scheuer
for his generous and compassionate heart
and for teaching me the etiquette of
being a gentleman

A LONG
WAY GONE

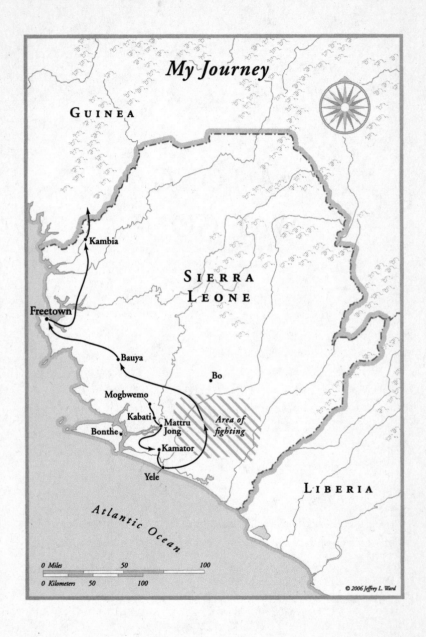

New York City, 1998

MY HIGH SCHOOL FRIENDS have begun to suspect I haven't told them the full story of my life.

"Why did you leave Sierra Leone?"

"Because there is a war."

"Did you witness some of the fighting?"

"Everyone in the country did."

"You mean you saw people running around with guns and shooting each other?"

"Yes, all the time."

"Cool."

I smile a little.

"You should tell us about it sometime."

"Yes, sometime."

1

---◆◆◆---

THERE WERE ALL KINDS of stories told about the war that made it sound as if it was happening in a faraway and different land. It wasn't until refugees started passing through our town that we began to see that it was actually taking place in our country. Families who had walked hundreds of miles told how relatives had been killed and their houses burned. Some people felt sorry for them and offered them places to stay, but most of the refugees refused, because they said the war would eventually reach our town. The children of these families wouldn't look at us, and they jumped at the sound of chopping wood or as stones landed on the tin roofs flung by children hunting birds with slingshots. The adults among these children from the war zones would be lost in their thoughts during conversations with the elders of my town. Apart from their fatigue and malnourishment, it was evident they had seen something that plagued their minds, something that we would refuse to accept if they told us all of it. At times I thought that some of the stories the passersby told were exaggerated. The only wars I knew of were those that I had read about in books or seen in movies such as *Rambo: First Blood*, and the one in neighboring Liberia that I had heard about on the BBC news. My imagination at ten years old didn't have the capacity to grasp what had taken away the happiness of the refugees.

The first time that I was touched by war I was twelve. It was in January of 1993. I left home with Junior, my older brother, and our friend Talloi, both a year older than I, to go to the town of Mattru Jong, to participate in our friends' talent show. Mohamed, my best friend, couldn't come because he and his father were renovating their thatched-roof kitchen that day. The four of us had started a rap and dance group when I was eight. We were first introduced to rap music during one of our visits to Mobimbi, a quarter where the foreigners who worked for the same American company as my father lived. We often went to Mobimbi to swim in a pool and watch the huge color television and the white people who crowded the visitors' recreational area. One evening a music video that consisted of a bunch of young black fellows talking really fast came on the television. The four of us sat there mesmerized by the song, trying to understand what the black fellows were saying. At the end of the video, some letters came up at the bottom of the screen. They read "Sugarhill Gang, 'Rapper's Delight.'" Junior quickly wrote it down on a piece of paper. After that, we came to the quarters every other weekend to study that kind of music on television. We didn't know what it was called then, but I was impressed with the fact that the black fellows knew how to speak English really fast, and to the beat.

Later on, when Junior went to secondary school, he befriended some boys who taught him more about foreign music and dance. During holidays, he brought me cassettes and taught my friends and me how to dance to what we came to know as hip-hop. I loved the dance, and particularly enjoyed learning the lyrics, because they were poetic and it improved my vocabulary. One afternoon, Father came home while Junior, Mohamed, Talloi, and I were learning the verse of "I Know You Got Soul" by Eric B. & Rakim. He stood by the door of our clay brick and tin roof house laughing and then asked, "Can you even understand what you are saying?" He left before Junior could answer. He sat in a hammock under the shade of the mango, guava, and orange trees and tuned his radio to the BBC news.

"Now, this is good English, the kind that you should be listening to," he shouted from the yard.

While Father listened to the news, Junior taught us how to move our feet to the beat. We alternately moved our right and then our left feet to the front and back, and simultaneously did the same with our arms, shaking our upper bodies and heads. "This move is called the running man," Junior said. Afterward, we would practice miming the rap songs we had memorized. Before we parted to carry out our various evening chores of fetching water and cleaning lamps, we would say "Peace, son" or "I'm out," phrases we had picked up from the rap lyrics. Outside, the evening music of birds and crickets would commence.

On the morning that we left for Mattru Jong, we loaded our backpacks with notebooks of lyrics we were working on and stuffed our pockets with cassettes of rap albums. In those days we wore baggy jeans, and underneath them we had soccer shorts and sweatpants for dancing. Under our long-sleeved shirts we had sleeveless undershirts, T-shirts, and soccer jerseys. We wore three pairs of socks that we pulled down and folded to make our *crapes** look puffy. When it got too hot in the day, we took some of the clothes off and carried them on our shoulders. They were fashionable, and we had no idea that this unusual way of dressing was going to benefit us. Since we intended to return the next day, we didn't say goodbye or tell anyone where we were going. We didn't know that we were leaving home, never to return.

To save money, we decided to walk the sixteen miles to Mattru Jong. It was a beautiful summer day, the sun wasn't too hot, and the walk didn't feel long either, as we chatted about all kinds of things, mocked and chased each other. We carried slingshots that we used

*Sneakers.

to stone birds and chase the monkeys that tried to cross the main dirt road. We stopped at several rivers to swim. At one river that had a bridge across it, we heard a passenger vehicle in the distance and decided to get out of the water and see if we could catch a free ride. I got out before Junior and Talloi, and ran across the bridge with their clothes. They thought they could catch up with me before the vehicle reached the bridge, but upon realizing that it was impossible, they started running back to the river, and just when they were in the middle of the bridge, the vehicle caught up to them. The girls in the truck laughed and the driver tapped his horn. It was funny, and for the rest of the trip they tried to get me back for what I had done, but they failed.

We arrived at Kabati, my grandmother's village, around two in the afternoon. Mamie Kpana was the name that my grandmother was known by. She was tall and her perfectly long face complemented her beautiful cheekbones and big brown eyes. She always stood with her hands either on her hips or on her head. By looking at her, I could see where my mother had gotten her beautiful dark skin, extremely white teeth, and the translucent creases on her neck. My grandfather or kamor—teacher, as everyone called him—was a well-known local Arabic scholar and healer in the village and beyond.

At Kabati, we ate, rested a bit, and started the last six miles. Grandmother wanted us to spend the night, but we told her that we would be back the following day.

"How is that father of yours treating you these days?" she asked in a sweet voice that was laden with worry.

"Why are you going to Mattru Jong, if not for school? And why do you look so skinny?" she continued asking, but we evaded her questions. She followed us to the edge of the village and watched as we descended the hill, switching her walking stick to her left hand so that she could wave us off with her right hand, a sign of good luck.

We arrived in Mattru Jong a couple of hours later and met up with old friends, Gibrilla, Kaloko, and Khalilou. That night we went out to Bo Road, where street vendors sold food late into the night. We bought boiled groundnut and ate it as we conversed about what we were going to do the next day, made plans to see the space for the talent show and practice. We stayed in the verandah room of Khalilou's house. The room was small and had a tiny bed, so the four of us (Gibrilla and Kaloko went back to their houses) slept in the same bed, lying across with our feet hanging. I was able to fold my feet in a little more since I was shorter and smaller than all the other boys.

The next day Junior, Talloi, and I stayed at Khalilou's house and waited for our friends to return from school at around 2:00 p.m. But they came home early. I was cleaning my *crapes* and counting for Junior and Talloi, who were having a push-up competition. Gibrilla and Kaloko walked onto the verandah and joined the competition. Talloi, breathing hard and speaking slowly, asked why they were back. Gibrilla explained that the teachers had told them that the rebels had attacked Mogbwemo, our home. School had been canceled until further notice. We stopped what we were doing.

According to the teachers, the rebels had attacked the mining areas in the afternoon. The sudden outburst of gunfire had caused people to run for their lives in different directions. Fathers had come running from their workplaces, only to stand in front of their empty houses with no indication of where their families had gone. Mothers wept as they ran toward schools, rivers, and water taps to look for their children. Children ran home to look for parents who were wandering the streets in search of them. And as the gunfire intensified, people gave up looking for their loved ones and ran out of town.

"This town will be next, according to the teachers." Gibrilla lifted himself from the cement floor. Junior, Talloi, and I took our backpacks and headed to the wharf with our friends. There, people were arriving from all over the mining area. Some we knew, but they couldn't tell us the whereabouts of our families. They said the attack had been too sudden, too chaotic; that everyone had fled in different directions in total confusion.

For more than three hours, we stayed at the wharf, anxiously waiting and expecting either to see our families or to talk to someone who

But there was no news of them, and after a while we ~~~ of the people who came across the river. The day ~~~ normal. The sun peacefully sailed through the white ~~~, birds sang from treetops, the trees danced to the quiet wind. I still couldn't believe that the war had actually reached our home. It is impossible, I thought. When we left home the day before, there had been no indication the rebels were anywhere near.

"What are you going to do?" Gibrilla asked us. We were all quiet for a while, and then Talloi broke the silence. "We must go back and see if we can find our families before it is too late."

Junior and I nodded in agreement.

Just three days earlier, I had seen my father walking slowly from work. His hard hat was under his arm and his long face was sweating from the hot afternoon sun. I was sitting on the verandah. I had not seen him for a while, as another stepmother had destroyed our relationship again. But that morning my father smiled at me as he came up the steps. He examined my face, and his lips were about to utter something, when my stepmother came out. He looked away, then at my stepmother, who pretended not to see me. They quietly went into the parlor. I held back my tears and left the verandah to meet with Junior at the junction where we waited for the lorry. We were on our way to see our mother in the next town about three miles away. When our father had paid for our school, we had seen her on weekends over the holidays when we were back home. Now that he refused to pay, we visited her every two or three days. That afternoon we met Mother at the market and walked with her as she purchased ingredients to cook for us. Her face was dull at first, but as soon as she hugged us, she brightened up. She told us that our little brother, Ibrahim, was at school and that we would go get him on our way from the market. She held our hands as we walked, and every so often she would turn around as if to see whether we were still with her.

As we walked to our little brother's school, Mother turned to us and said, "I am sorry I do not have enough money to put you boys back in school at this point. I am working on it." She paused and then asked, "How is your father these days?"

"He seems all right. I saw him this afternoon," I replied. Junior didn't say anything.

Mother looked him directly in the eyes and said, "Your father is a good man and he loves you very much. He just seems to attract the wrong stepmothers for you boys."

When we got to the school, our little brother was in the yard playing soccer with his friends. He was eight and pretty good for his age. As soon as he saw us, he came running, throwing himself on us. He measured himself against me to see if he had gotten taller than me. Mother laughed. My little brother's small round face glowed, and sweat formed around the creases he had on his neck, just like my mother's. All four of us walked to Mother's house. I held my little brother's hand, and he told me about school and challenged me to a soccer game later in the evening. My mother was single and devoted herself to taking care of Ibrahim. She said he sometimes asked about our father. When Junior and I were away in school, she had taken Ibrahim to see him a few times, and each time she had cried when my father hugged Ibrahim, because they were both so happy to see each other. My mother seemed lost in her thoughts, smiling as she relived the moments.

Two days after that visit, we had left home. As we now stood at the wharf in Mattru Jong, I could visualize my father holding his hard hat and running back home from work, and my mother, weeping and running to my little brother's school. A sinking feeling overtook me.

Junior, Talloi, and I jumped into a canoe and sadly waved to our friends as the canoe pulled away from the shores of Mattru Jong. As we landed on the other side of the river, more and more people were arriving in haste. We started walking, and a woman carrying her flip-flops on her head spoke without looking at us: "Too much blood has been spilled where you are going. Even the good spirits have fled from that place." She walked past us. In the bushes along the river, the strained voices of women cried out, "*Nguwor gbor mu ma oo,*" God help us, and screamed the names of their children: "Yusufu, Jabu, Foday . . ." We saw children walking by themselves, shirtless, in their underwear, following the crowd. "*Nya nje oo, nya keke oo,*" my mother, my father, the children were crying. There were also dogs running, in between the crowds of people, who were still running, even though far away from harm. The dogs sniffed the air, looking for their owners. My veins tightened.

We had walked six miles and were now at Kabati, Grandmother's village. It was deserted. All that was left were footprints in the sand leading toward the dense forest that spread out beyond the village.

As evening approached, people started arriving from the mining area. Their whispers, the cries of little children seeking lost parents and tired of walking, and the wails of hungry babies replaced the evening songs of crickets and birds. We sat on Grandmother's verandah, waiting and listening.

"Do you guys think it is a good idea to go back to Mogbwemo?" Junior asked. But before either of us had a chance to answer, a Volkswagen roared in the distance and all the people walking on the road ran into the nearby bushes. We ran, too, but didn't go that far. My heart pounded and my breathing intensified. The vehicle stopped in front of my grandmother's house, and from where we lay, we could see that whoever was inside the car was not armed. As we, and others, emerged from the bushes, we saw a man run from the driver's seat to the sidewalk, where he vomited blood. His arm was bleeding. When he stopped vomiting, he began to cry. It was the first time I had seen a grown man cry like a child, and I felt a sting in my heart. A woman put her arms around the man and begged him to stand up. He got to his feet and walked toward the van. When he opened the door opposite the driver's, a woman who was leaning against it fell to the ground. Blood was coming out of her ears. People covered the eyes of their children.

In the back of the van were three more dead bodies, two girls and a boy, and their blood was all over the seats and the ceiling of the van. I wanted to move away from what I was seeing, but couldn't. My feet went numb and my entire body froze. Later we learned that the man had tried to escape with his family and the rebels had shot at his vehicle, killing all his family. The only thing that consoled him, for a few seconds at least, was when the woman who had embraced him, and now cried with him, told him that at least he would have the chance to bury them. He would always know where they were laid to rest, she said. She seemed to know a little more about war than the rest of us.

The wind had stopped moving and daylight seemed to be quickly giving in to night. As sunset neared, more people passed through the village. One man carried his dead son. He thought the boy was still alive. The father was covered with his son's blood, and as he ran he kept saying, "I will get you to the hospital, my boy, and everything will be fine." Perhaps it was necessary that he cling to false hopes, since they kept him running away from harm. A group of men and women who had been pierced by stray bullets came running next. The skin that hung down from their bodies still contained fresh blood. Some of them didn't notice that they were wounded until they stopped and people pointed to their wounds. Some fainted or vomited. I felt nauseated, and my head was spinning. I felt the ground moving, and people's voices seemed to be far removed from where I stood trembling.

The last casualty that we saw that evening was a woman who carried her baby on her back. Blood was running down her dress and dripping behind her, making a trail. Her child had been shot dead as she ran for her life. Luckily for her, the bullet didn't go through the baby's body. When she stopped at where we stood, she sat on the ground and removed her child. It was a girl, and her eyes were still open, with an interrupted innocent smile on her face. The bullets could be seen sticking out just a little bit in the baby's body and she was swelling. The mother clung to her child and rocked her. She was in too much pain and shock to shed tears.

Junior, Talloi, and I looked at each other and knew that we must return to Mattru Jong, because we had seen that Mogbwemo was no longer a place to call home and that our parents couldn't possibly be there anymore. Some of the wounded people kept saying that Kabati was next on the rebels' list. We didn't want to be there when the rebels arrived. Even those who couldn't walk very well did their best to keep moving away from Kabati. The image of that woman and her baby plagued my mind as we walked back to Mattru Jong. I barely noticed the journey, and when I drank water I didn't feel any relief even though I knew I was thirsty. I didn't want to go back to where that woman was from; it was clear in the eyes of the baby that all had been lost.

"You were negative nineteen years old." That's what my father used to say when I would ask about what life was like in Sierra Leone following independence in 1961. It had been a British colony since 1808. Sir Milton Margai became the first prime minister and ruled the country under the Sierra Leone Peoples Party (SLPP) political banner until his death in 1964. His half brother Sir Albert Margai succeeded him until 1967, when Siaka Stevens, the All People's Congress (APC) Party leader, won the election, which was followed by a military coup. Siaka Stevens returned to power in 1968, and several years later declared the country a one-party state, the APC being the sole legal party. It was the beginning of "rotten politics," as my father would put it. I wondered what he would say about the war that I was now running from. I had heard from adults that this was a revolutionary war, a liberation of the people from corrupt government. But what kind of liberation movement shoots innocent civilians, children, that little girl? There wasn't anyone to answer these questions, and my head felt heavy with the images that it contained. As we walked, I became afraid of the road, the mountains in the distance, and the bushes on either side.

We arrived in Mattru Jong late that night. Junior and Talloi explained to our friends what we had seen, while I stayed quiet, still trying to decide whether what I had seen was real. That night, when I finally managed to drift off, I dreamt that I was shot in my side and people ran past me without helping, as they were all running for their lives. I tried to crawl to safety in the bushes, but from out of nowhere there was someone standing on top of me with a gun. I couldn't make out his face as the sun was against it. That person pointed the gun at the place where I had been shot and pulled the trigger. I woke up and hesitantly touched my side. I became afraid, since I could no longer tell the difference between dream and reality.

Every morning in Mattru Jong we would go down to the wharf for news from home. But after a week the stream of refugees from that direction ceased and news dried up. Government troops were deployed in Mattru Jong, and they erected checkpoints at the wharf and other strategic locations all over town. The soldiers were convinced that if the rebels attacked, they would come from across the river, so they mounted heavy artillery there and announced a 7:00 p.m. curfew, which made the nights tense, as we couldn't sleep and had to be inside too early. During the day, Gibrilla and Kaloko came over. The six of us sat on the verandah and discussed what was going on.

"I do not think that this madness will last," Junior said quietly. He looked at me as if to assure me that we would soon go home.

"It will probably last for only a month or two." Talloi stared at the floor.

"I heard that the soldiers are already on their way to get the rebels out of the mining areas," Gibrilla stammered. We agreed that the war was just a passing phase that wouldn't last over three months.

Junior, Talloi, and I listened to rap music, trying to memorize the lyrics so that we could avoid thinking about the situation at hand. Naughty by Nature, LL Cool J, Run-D.M.C., and Heavy D & The Boyz; we had left home with only these cassettes and the clothes that we wore. I remember sitting on the verandah listening to "Now That We Found Love" by Heavy D & The Boyz and watching the trees at the edge of town that reluctantly moved to the slow wind. The palms beyond them were still, as if awaiting something. I closed my eyes, and the images from Kabati flashed in my mind. I tried to drive them out by evoking older memories of Kabati before the war.

There was a thick forest on one side of the village where my grand-mother lived and coffee farms on the other. A river flowed from the forest to the edge of the village, passing through palm kernels into a swamp. Above the swamp banana farms stretched into the horizon. The main dirt road that passed through Kabati was rutted with holes and puddles where ducks liked to bathe during the day, and in the backyards of the houses birds nested in mango trees.

In the morning, the sun would rise from behind the forest. First, its rays penetrated through the leaves, and gradually, with cockcrows and sparrows that vigorously proclaimed daylight, the golden sun sat at the top of the forest. In the evening, monkeys could be seen in the forest jumping from tree to tree, returning to their sleeping places. On the coffee farms, chickens were always busy hiding their young from hawks. Beyond the farms, palm trees waved their fronds with the moving wind. Sometimes a palm wine tapper could be seen climbing in the early evening.

The evening ended with the cracking of branches in the forest and the pounding of rice in mortars. The echoes resonated in the village, causing birds to fly off and return curiously chattering. Crickets, frogs, toads, and owls followed them, all calling for night while leaving their hiding places. Smoke rose from thatched-roof kitchens, and people would start arriving from farms carrying lamps and sometimes lit firewood.

"We must strive to be like the moon." An old man in Kabati re-peated this sentence often to people who walked past his house on their way to the river to fetch water, to hunt, to tap palm wine; and to their farms. I remember asking my grandmother what the old man meant. She explained that the adage served to remind people to always be on their best behavior and to be good to others. She said that peo-ple complain when there is too much sun and it gets unbearably hot, and also when it rains too much or when it is cold. But, she said, no one grumbles when the moon shines. Everyone becomes happy and appreciates the moon in their own special way. Children watch their shadows and play in its light, people gather at the square to tell stories and dance through the night. A lot of happy things happen when the moon shines. These are some of the reasons why we should want to be like the moon.

"You look hungry. I will fix you some cassava." She ended the discussion.

After my grandmother told me why we should strive to be like the moon, I took it upon myself to closely observe it. Each night when the moon appeared in the sky, I would lie on the ground outside and quietly watch it. I wanted to find out why it was so appealing and likable. I became fascinated with the different shapes that I saw inside the moon. Some nights I saw the head of a man. He had a medium beard and wore a sailor's hat. Other times I saw a man with an ax chopping wood, and sometimes a woman cradling a baby at her breast. Whenever I get a chance to observe the moon now, I still see those same images I saw when I was six, and it pleases me to know that that part of my childhood is still embedded in me.

2

I AM PUSHING a rusty wheelbarrow in a town where the air smells of blood and burnt flesh. The breeze brings the faint cries of those whose last breaths are leaving their mangled bodies. I walk past them. Their arms and legs are missing; their intestines spill out through the bullet holes in their stomachs; brain matter comes out of their noses and ears. The flies are so excited and intoxicated that they fall on the pools of blood and die. The eyes of the nearly dead are redder than the blood that comes out of them, and it seems that their bones will tear through the skin of their taut faces at any minute. I turn my face to the ground to look at my feet. My tattered *crapes* are soaked with blood, which seems to be running down my army shorts. I feel no physical pain, so I am not sure whether I've been wounded. I can feel the warmth of my AK-47's barrel on my back; I don't remember when I last fired it. It feels as if needles have been hammered into my brain, and it is hard to be sure whether it is day or night. The wheelbarrow in front of me contains a dead body wrapped in white bedsheets. I do not know why I am taking this particular body to the cemetery.

When I arrive at the cemetery, I struggle to lift it from the wheelbarrow; it feels as if the body is resisting. I carry it in my arms, looking for a suitable place to lay it to rest. My body begins to ache and I can't lift a foot without feeling a rush of pain from my toes to my spine. I collapse on the ground and hold the body in my arms. Blood spots begin to emerge on the white bedsheets covering it. Setting the body on the ground, I start to unwrap it, beginning at the feet. All the way up to the neck, there are bullet holes. One bullet has crushed the Adam's apple and sent the remains of it to the back of the throat. I lift the cloth from the body's face. I am looking at my own.

I lay sweating for a few minutes on the cool wooden floor where I had fallen, before turning on the light so that I could completely free myself from the dreamworld. A piercing pain ran through my spine. I studied the red exposed brick wall of the room and tried to identify the rap music coming from a car passing by. A shudder racked my body, and I tried to think about my new life in New York City, where I had been for over a month. But my mind wandered across the Atlantic Ocean back to Sierra Leone. I saw myself holding an AK-47 and walking through a coffee farm with a squad that consisted of many boys and a few adults. We were on our way to attack a small town that had ammunition and food. As soon as we left the coffee farm, we unexpectedly ran into another armed group at a soccer field adjoining the ruins of what had once been a village. We opened fire until the last living being in the other group fell to the ground. We walked toward the dead bodies, giving each other high fives. The group had also consisted of young boys like us, but we didn't care about them. We took their ammunition, sat on their bodies, and started eating the cooked food they had been carrying. All around us, fresh blood leaked from the bullet holes in their bodies.

I got up from the floor, soaked a white towel with a glass of water, and tied it around my head. I was afraid to fall asleep, but staying awake also brought back painful memories. Memories I sometimes wish I could wash away, even though I am aware that they are an important part of what my life is; who I am now. I stayed awake all night, anxiously waiting for daylight, so that I could fully return to my new life, to rediscover the happiness I had known as a child, the joy that had stayed alive inside me even through times when being alive itself became a burden. These days I live in three worlds: my dreams, and the experiences of my new life, which trigger memories from the past.

3

We were in Mattru Jong longer than we had anticipated. We hadn't heard any news about our families and didn't know what else to do except wait and hope that they were well.

We heard that the rebels were stationed in Sumbuya, a town twenty or so miles to the northeast of Mattru Jong. This rumor was soon replaced by letters brought by people whose lives the rebels had spared during their massacre in Sumbuya. The letters simply informed the people of Mattru Jong that the rebels were coming and wanted to be welcomed, since they were fighting for us. One of the messengers was a young man. They had carved their initials, RUF (Revolutionary United Front), on his body with a hot bayonet and chopped off all his fingers with the exception of his thumbs. The rebels called this mutilation "one love." Before the war, people raised a thumb to say "One love" to each other, an expression popularized by the love and influence of reggae music.

When people received the message from the miserable messenger, they went into hiding in the forest that very night. But Khalilou's family had asked us to stay behind and follow them with the rest of

their property if things didn't improve in the subsequent days, so we
stayed put.

That night for the first time in my life I realized that it is the physical presence of people and their spirits that gives a town life. With
the absence of so many people, the town became scary, the night
darker, and the silence unbearably agitating. Normally, the crickets
and birds sang in the evening before the sun went down. But this
time they didn't, and darkness set in very fast. The moon wasn't in
the sky; the air was stiff, as if nature itself was afraid of what was
happening.

The majority of the town's population was in hiding for a week, and
more people went into hiding after the arrival of more messengers. But
the rebels didn't come on the day they said they would, and as a result,
people started moving back into the town. As soon as everyone was
settled again, another message was sent. This time the messenger was
a well-known Catholic bishop who had been doing missionary work
when he ran into the rebels. They didn't do anything to the bishop except threaten that if he failed to deliver their message they would come
for him. Upon receiving the word, people again left town and headed
for their various hiding places in the forests. And we were again left behind, this time not to carry Khalilou's family's belongings, as we had
already taken them into hiding, but to look after the house and to buy
certain food products like salt, pepper, rice, and fish that we took to
Khalilou's family in the bush.

Another ten days of hiding, and still the rebels hadn't arrived. There
was nothing to do but conclude that they weren't coming. The town
came alive again. Schools reopened; people returned to their normal
routines. Five days went by peacefully, and even the soldiers in town
relaxed.

I would sometimes go for walks by myself in the late evening. The
sight of women preparing dinner always reminded me of the times I
used to watch my mother cook. Boys weren't allowed in the kitchen,
but she made an exception for me, saying, "You need to know how to

cook something for your *palampo** life." She would pause, give me a piece of dry fish, and then continue: "I want a grandchild. So don't be a *palampo* forever." Tears would form in my eyes as I continued my stroll on the tiny gravel roads in Mattru Jong.

When the rebels finally came, I was cooking. The rice was done and the okra soup was almost ready when I heard a single gunshot that echoed through the town. Junior, Talloi, Kaloko, Gibrilla, and Khalilou, who were in the room, ran outside. "Did you hear that?" they asked. We stood still, trying to determine whether the soldiers had fired the shot. A minute later, three different guns rapidly went off. This time we started to get worried. "It is just the soldiers testing their weapons," one of our friends assured us. The town became very quiet, and no gunshots were heard for more than fifteen minutes. I went back to the kitchen and started to dish out the rice. At that instant several gunshots, which sounded like thunder striking the tin-roofed houses, took over town. The sound of the guns was so terrifying it confused everyone. No one was able to think clearly. In a matter of seconds, people started screaming and running in different directions, pushing and trampling on whoever had fallen on the ground. No one had the time to take anything with them. Everyone just ran to save his or her life. Mothers lost their children, whose confused, sad cries coincided with the gunshots. Families were separated and left behind everything they had worked for their whole lives. My heart was beating faster than it ever had. Each gunshot seemed to cling to the beat of my heart.

The rebels fired their guns toward the sky, as they shouted and merrily danced their way into town in a semicircle formation. There are two ways to enter Mattru Jong. One is by road and the other by crossing the river Jong. The rebels attacked and advanced into the town from inland, forcing the civilians to run toward the river. A lot of people were so terrified that they just ran to the river, jumped in, and lost the strength to swim. The soldiers, who somehow anticipated the

*Single.

attack and knew they were outnumbered, left town before the rebels
actually came. This was a surprise to Junior, Talloi, Khalilou, Gibrilla,
Kaloko, and me, whose initial instinct was to run to where the soldiers
were stationed. We stood there, in front of mounted sandbags, unable
to decide which way to go next. We started running again toward
where there were fewer gunshots.

There was only one escape route out of town. Everyone headed for
it. Mothers were screaming the names of their lost children, and the
lost children cried in vain. We ran together, trying to keep up with
each other. In order to get to the escape route, we had to cross a wet
and muddy swamp that was adjacent to a tiny hill. In the swamp we
ran past people who were stuck in the mud, past handicapped people
who couldn't be helped, for anyone who stopped to do so was risking
his own life.

After we crossed the swamp, the real trouble started, because the
rebels began shooting their guns at people instead of shooting into the
sky. They didn't want people to abandon the town, because they
needed to use civilians as a shield against the military. One of the main
aims of the rebels when they took over a town was to force the civilians
to stay with them, especially women and children. This way they
could stay longer, as military intervention would be delayed.

We were now at the top of a bushy hill immediately behind the
swamp, in a clearing just before the escape route. Seeing the civilians
all about to make it out, the rebels fired rocket-propelled grenades
(RPGs), machine guns, AK-47s, G3s, all the weapons they had, directly into the clearing. But we knew we had no choice, we had to
make it across the clearing because, as young boys, the risk of staying
in town was greater for us than trying to escape. Young boys were
immediately recruited, and the initials RUF were carved wherever it
pleased the rebels, with a hot bayonet. This not only meant that you
were scarred for life but that you could never escape from them, because escaping with the carving of the rebels' initials was asking for
death, as soldiers would kill you without any questions and militant
civilians would do the same.

We dodged from bush to bush and made it to the other side. But this was just the beginning of many risky situations that were to come. Immediately after one explosion, we got up and ran together, with our heads down, jumping over fresh dead bodies and flames of burnt dried trees. We were almost at the end of the clearing when we heard the whizzing of another rocket grenade approaching. We sped up our steps and took dives into the bush before the grenade landed, followed by several rounds of machine gun fire. The people who were right behind us were not as lucky as we were. The RPG caught up with them. One of them caught the fragments of the RPG. He cried out loudly and screamed that he was blind. No one dared to go out and help him. He was halted by another grenade that exploded, causing his remains and blood to sprinkle like rain on the nearby leaves and bushes. All of it happened too fast.

As soon as we had crossed the clearing, the rebels sent some of their men to catch those who had made it into the bush. They started chasing and shooting after us. We ran for more than an hour without stopping. It was unbelievable how fast and long we ran. I didn't sweat or get tired at all. Junior was in front of me and behind Talloi. Every few seconds, my brother would call my name, to make sure I wasn't left behind. I could hear the sadness in his voice, and each time I answered him, my voice trembled. Gibrilla, Kaloko, and Khalilou were behind me. Their breathing was heavy and I could hear one of them hissing, trying not to cry. Talloi was a very fast runner, even when we were younger. But on that evening we were able to keep up with him. After an hour or maybe even more of running, the rebels gave up the chase and returned to Mattru Jong while we continued on.

4

FOR SEVERAL DAYS the six of us walked on a tiny path that was about a foot wide, walled by thick bushes on either side. Junior was in front of me and his hands didn't swing as they used to when he strolled across the yard on his way back from school. I wanted to know what he was thinking, but everyone was too quiet and I didn't know how to break the silence. I thought about where my family was, whether I would be able to see them again, and wished that they were safe and not too heartbroken about Junior and me. Tears formed in my eyes, but I was too hungry to cry.

We slept in abandoned villages, where we lay on the bare ground and hoped that the following day we would be able to find something other than raw cassava to eat. We had passed through a village that had banana, orange, and coconut trees. Khalilou, who knew how to climb better than all of us, mounted each of those trees and plucked as much from them as he could. The bananas were raw, so we boiled them by adding wood to a fire that was in one of the outdoor kitchens. Some-one must have left that village when he or she saw us coming, because the fire was new. The bananas didn't taste good at all, because there was no salt or any other ingredients, but we ate every single bit, just to have something in our stomachs. Afterward, we ate some oranges and some coconuts. We could not find something substantial to eat. We got hungrier day after day, to the point that our stomachs were hurting and our visions blurred at times. We had no choice but to sneak back into Mattru Jong, along with some people we encountered on the path, to get some money we had left behind, so that we could buy food.

On our way through the quiet and almost barren town, which now seemed unfamiliar, we saw rotten pots of food that had been left behind. Bodies, furniture, clothes, and all kinds of property were scattered all over. On one verandah we saw an old man sitting in a chair as if asleep. There was a bullet hole in his forehead, and underneath the stoop lay the bodies of two men whose genitals, limbs, and hands had been chopped off by a machete that was on the ground next to their piled body parts. I vomited and immediately felt feverish, but we had to continue on. We ran on tiptoe as fast and as cautiously as we could, avoiding the main streets. We stood against walls of houses and inspected the tiny gravel roads between houses before crossing to another house. At one point, as soon as we had crossed the road, we heard footsteps. There was no immediate cover, so we had to swiftly run onto a verandah and hide behind stacks of cement bricks. We peeped from behind the bricks and saw two rebels who wore baggy jeans, *sleepers*,* and white T-shirts. Their heads were tied with red handkerchiefs and they carried their guns behind their backs. They were escorting a group of young women who carried cooking pots, bags of rice, mortars and pestles. We watched them until they were out of sight before we began moving again. We finally got to Khalilou's house. All the doors were broken and the house was torn apart. The house, like every other in the town, had been looted. There was a bullet hole in the doorframe and broken glasses of Star beer, a popular brand in the country, and empty cigarette packets on the verandah floor. There was nothing of use to be found in the house. The only food that was

*Flip-flops.

available was raw rice in bags that were too heavy to carry and would slow us down. But the money was, luckily, still where I had kept it, which was in a tiny plastic bag under the foot of the bed. I put it inside my *crape*, and we headed back toward the swamp.

The six of us, including the people we had entered the town together with, gathered at the edge of the swamp as planned and started crossing the clearing three at a time. I was in the second batch, with Talloi and another person. We started to crawl across the clearing at the signal of the first group that had made it across. While we were in the middle of the clearing, they signaled for us to lie flat, and as soon as we hit the ground, they motioned for us to continue crawling. There were dead bodies everywhere and flies were feasting on the congealed blood on them. After we made it to the other side, we saw that there were rebels on guard in a little tower at the wharf that overlooked the clearing. The next batch was Junior and two others. As they were crossing, something fell out of someone's pocket onto an aluminum pan in the clearing. The sound was loud enough to get the attention of the rebels on guard, and they pointed their guns toward where the sound had come from. My heart throbbed with pain as I watched my brother lying on the ground, pretending to be one of the dead bodies. Several shots were heard in town, and that distracted the rebels and made them turn the other way. Junior and the two others made it. His face was dusty and there were residues of mud in between his teeth. He breathed heavily, clenching his fists. One boy among the last batch to cross the clearing was too slow, because he carried a big bag of things he had gathered from his house. As a result, the rebels who were on guard in the little tower saw him and opened fire. Some of the rebels underneath the tower started running and shooting toward us. We whispered to the boy, "Drop the bag and hurry. The rebels are coming. Come on." But the boy didn't listen. It fell from his shoulder after he had crossed the clearing, and as we ran away, I saw him pulling on the bag, which was stuck between tree stumps. We ran as fast as we could until we lost the rebels. It was sunset and we walked quietly toward the big red sun and the still sky that awaited darkness. The boy who

caused the rebels to spot us didn't make it to the first crowded village
we reached.

That night we were temporarily happy that we had some money,
and were hoping to buy some cooked rice with cassava or potato leaves
for dinner. We high-fived each other as we approached the village market, and our stomachs growled as the smell of palm oil wafted from
cooking huts. But when we got back to the cooked-food stalls, we were
disappointed to find that those who had been selling cassava leaves,
okra soup, and potato leaves, all cooked with dried fish and rich palm
oil served with rice, had ceased to do so. Some of them were saving
their food in case things got worse, and others simply didn't want to
sell any more for unexplained reasons.

After all the trouble and risk we undertook to get the money, it became useless. We would have been less hungry if we had stayed at the
village instead of walking the miles to Mattru Jong and back. I wanted
to blame someone for this particular predicament, but there was no
one to be blamed. We had made a logical decision and it had come to
this. It was a typical aspect of being in the war. Things changed rapidly
in a matter of seconds and no one had any control over anything. We
had yet to learn these things and implement survival tactics, which was
what it came down to. That night we were so hungry that we stole
people's food while they slept. It was the only way to get through the
night.

5

WE WERE SO HUNGRY that it hurt to drink water and we felt cramps in our guts. It was as though something were eating the insides of our stomachs. Our lips became parched and our joints weakened and ached. I began to feel my ribs when I touched my sides. We didn't know where else to get food. The one cassava farm that we ravaged didn't last long. Birds and animals such as rabbits were nowhere to be seen. We became irritable and sat apart from each other, as if sitting together made us hungrier.

One evening we actually chased a little boy who was eating two boiled ears of corn by himself. He was about five years old and was enjoying the corn that he held in both hands, taking turns biting each ear. We didn't say a word or even look at each other. Rather, we rushed on the boy at the same time, and before he knew what was happening, we had taken the corn from him. We shared it among the six of us and ate our little portion while the boy cried and ran to his parents. The boy's parents didn't confront us about the incident. I guess they knew that six boys would jump on their son for two ears of corn only if they were desperately hungry. Later in the evening, the boy's mother gave

each of us an ear of corn. I felt guilty about it for a few minutes, but in
our position, there wasn't much time for remorse.

I do not know the name of the village that we were in and didn't
bother to ask, since I was busy trying to survive the everyday obstacles.
We didn't know the names of other towns and villages and how to get
there. So hunger drove us back to Mattru Jong again. It was dangerous, but hunger made us not care that much. It was summertime, the
dry season, and the grassland had grown yellowish. A fresh green forest engulfed it.

We were in the middle of the grassland walking in single file, our shirts
on our shoulders or heads, when suddenly three rebels rose from behind the dried grasses and pointed their guns at Gibrilla, who was in
the front. They cocked their guns, and one of them placed the muzzle
of his gun under Gibrilla's chin. "He is scared like a soaked monkey,"
the rebel laughingly told his companions. As the other two walked
past me, I avoided eye contact by putting my head down. The younger
rebel raised my head with his bayonet, still in its scabbard. While he
was looking at me sternly, he took the bayonet from its scabbard and
attached it at the muzzle of his gun. I trembled so hard that my lips
shook. He smiled without emotion. The rebels, none of whom were
older than twenty-one, started walking us back to a village we had
passed. One was dressed in a sleeveless army shirt and jeans, his head
tied with a red cloth. The other two were dressed in jeans jackets and
pants, wearing baseball hats backward and new Adidas sneakers. All
three wore a lot of fancy watches on both wrists. All these things had
been taken from people by force or looted from houses and shops.

The rebels said a lot of things as we walked. Whatever they said
didn't sound friendly. I couldn't hear their words, because all I could
think about was death. I struggled to avoid fainting.

As we approached the village, two of the rebels ran ahead. Six of us and
one rebel, I thought to myself. But he had a semiautomatic machine

gun and a long belt of bullets wrapped around him. He made us walk in two lines of three, with our hands on our heads. He was behind us, aiming his gun at our heads, and at some point he said, "If any of you makes a move, I will kill everyone. So don't even breathe too hard or it might be your last." He laughed and his voice echoed in the distant forest. I prayed that my friends and brother wouldn't make any sudden moves or even try to scratch an itch. The back of my head was getting warm, as if expecting a bullet anytime.

When we got to the village, the two rebels who had run ahead had gathered everyone who was there. There were over fifteen people, mostly young boys, some girls, and a few adults. They made us all stand in the compound of a house that was closer to the bush. It was getting dark. The rebels took out their big flashlights and placed them on top of the rice-pounding mortars, so that they could see everyone. While we stood there under gunpoint, an old man who had escaped from Mattru Jong was heard crossing a creaky wooden bridge leading to the village. While we watched, the youngest rebel walked toward the old man and waited for him at the foot of the bridge. He was placed at gunpoint as soon as he crossed over and brought in front of us. The man was probably in his sixties, but looked weak. His face was wrinkled from hunger and fear. The rebel pushed the old man to the ground, put a gun to his head, and ordered him to get up. On trembling knees the old man managed to stand. The rebels laughed at him and made us laugh with them by pointing their guns at us. I laughed loudly, but I was crying internally and my legs and hands trembled. I clenched my fists, but that made the trembling worse. All the captives stood at gunpoint watching as the rebels proceeded to interrogate the old man.

"Why did you leave Mattru Jong?" a rebel asked while examining his bayonet. He measured the length of his knife with his fingers and then held it against the old man's neck.

"It looks like a perfect fit." He motioned driving the bayonet through the old man's neck.

"Now are you going to answer my question?" The veins on his forehead stood out as his fierce red eyes watched the trembling face of the old man, whose eyelids were shaking uncontrollably. Before the war a young man wouldn't have dared to talk to anyone older in such a rude manner. We grew up in a culture that demanded good behavior from everyone, and especially from the young. Young people were required to respect their elders and everyone in the community.

"I left town to look for my family," the old man said in a frightened voice, as he managed to catch his breath. The rebel with the semiautomatic machine gun, who had been standing against a tree smoking a cigarette, furiously walked toward the old man and pointed his gun between the old man's legs.

"You left Mattru Jong because you don't like us." He put his gun on the old man's forehead and continued. "You left because you are against our cause as freedom fighters. Right?"

The old man closed his eyes tightly and began to sob.

What cause? I thought. I used the only freedom that I had then, my thought. They couldn't see it. While the interrogation went on, one of the rebels painted RUF on all the walls of the houses in the village. He was the sloppiest painter I have ever seen. I don't think he even knew his alphabet. Rather, he only knew what R, U, and F looked like. When he was done painting, he walked up to the old man and placed his gun to the old man's head.

"Do you have any last words to say?" The old man at this point was unable to speak. His lips trembled, but he couldn't get a word out. The rebel pulled the trigger, and like lightning, I saw the spark of fire that came from the muzzle. I turned my face to the ground. My knees started trembling and my heartbeat grew faster and louder. When I looked back, the old man was circling around like a dog trying to catch a fly on its tail. He kept screaming, "My head! My brains!" The rebels laughed at him. Finally, he stopped and slowly raised his hands toward his face like a person hesitant to look in a mirror. "I can see! I can hear!" he cried out, and fainted. It turned out that the rebels hadn't shot him but had fired at close range near his head. They were very amused at the old man's reaction.

The rebels now faced us and announced that they were going to select some people among us to be recruited, as it was the sole reason for
their patrol. They ordered everyone to line up: men, women, even
children younger than I. They walked up and down the line trying to
make eye contact with people. First, they chose Khalilou, and then
myself, then a few others. Each person that was chosen was asked to
stand in a different line facing the previous one. Junior wasn't chosen,
and I stood facing him on the other side of the crowd, on my way to
becoming a rebel. I looked at him, but he avoided eye contact, putting
his head down. It seemed as if our worlds were different now and our
connection was breaking. Fortunately, for some reason the rebels decided to do a fresh pick. One of them said that they had chosen
wrongly, since most of us who had been chosen were trembling and
that meant we were sissies.

"We want strong recruits, not weak ones." The rebel pushed us back
to the other side of the crowd. Junior edged next to me. He gave me a
soft poke. I looked up at him and he nodded and rubbed my head.

"Stand still for the final pick," one of the rebels screamed. Junior
stopped rubbing my head. During the second pick, Junior was chosen.
The rest of us weren't needed, so they escorted us to the river followed
by the chosen ones.

Sweeping an arm in our direction, one of the rebels announced,
"We are going to initiate all of you by killing these people in front of
you. We have to do this to show you blood and make you strong.
You'll never see any of these people again, unless you believe in life
after death." He punched his chest with his fist and laughed.

I turned around and looked at Junior, whose eyes were red because
he was trying to hold back his tears. He clenched his fists to keep his
hands from trembling. I began to cry quietly and all of a sudden felt
dizzy. One of the chosen boys vomited. A rebel pushed him to join us
by smashing him in the face with the butt of his gun. The boy's face
was bleeding as we continued on.

"Don't worry, guys, the next killing is on you," another rebel com-
mented, and laughed.

At the river they made us kneel and put our hands behind our heads. Suddenly loud gunshots not far away from the village were heard. Two of the rebels ran for cover behind the nearest trees; the other lay flat on the ground, aiming his gun toward the direction of the sound.

"Do you think they are . . ." The rebel on the ground was interrupted by more gunshots. The rebels began to fire back. Everyone scattered, running for their lives into the bushes. The rebels noticed what had happened and fired after us. I ran as fast as I could deep into the bush and lay flat on the ground behind a log. I could hear the gunshots coming closer, so I began to crawl farther into the bush. A bullet hit a tree directly above my head and fell on the ground next to me. I halted and held my breath. From where I lay, I saw the red bullets flying through the forest and into the night. I could hear my heart beat, and I had started breathing heavily, so I covered my nose to control it.

Some people were captured and I could hear them crying from whatever pain was being inflicted upon them. The sharp, harsh cry of a woman filled the forest, and I felt the fear in her voice piercing through my veins, causing my teeth to feel somehow sour. I crawled farther into the bush and found a place under a tree, where I lay for hours without moving. The rebels were still in the village, angrily cursing and shooting their guns. At some point they pretended to be gone, and someone who had escaped went back to the village. They captured him and I could hear them beating him. A few minutes later, gunshots were heard, followed by thick smoke that rose toward the sky. The forest was lit up by the fire that was set in the village.

It had been almost an hour and the rebels' gunshots had gradually faded. As I lay under the tree thinking of what to do next, I heard whispers from behind. At first I was afraid, but then I recognized the voices. It was Junior and my friends. They had somehow ended up running in the same direction. I was still a little hesitant to call them, so I waited just to be absolutely sure. "I think they are gone," I heard Junior whisper. I was so certain at this point that my voice involuntarily left me: "Junior, Talloi, Kaloko, Gibrilla, Khalilou. Is that you?" I spoke quickly. They got quieter. "Junior, can you hear me?" I called out again. "Yes, we are here by the rotten log," he replied. They guided me toward them. We then crawled closer to the village to get to the path. Once we found the path, we started walking back toward the village where we had spent most of our hunger days. Junior and I exchanged a look, and he gave me that smile he had held back when I was about to face death.

That night's journey was very quiet. None of us spoke. I knew we were walking, but I couldn't feel my feet touching the ground.

When we got to the village, we sat around the fire until dawn. Not a word was said. Everyone seemed to be in a different world or seemed to be pondering something. The following morning, we started speaking to each other as if awakened from a nightmare or a dream that had given us a different take on life and the situation we were in. We decided to leave the village the next day and go somewhere safe, somewhere far away from where we were. We had no idea where we would go or even how to get to a safe place, but we were determined to find one. During that day, we washed our clothes. We had no soap, so we just soaked them and put them out in the sun to dry while we sat naked in a nearby bush waiting for them to be ready. We had agreed to leave early in the morning of the next day.

6

BEING IN A GROUP of six boys was not to our advantage. But we needed to stay together because we had a better chance of escaping the day-to-day troubles we faced. People were terrified of boys our age. Some had heard rumors about young boys being forced by rebels to kill their families and burn their villages. These children now patrolled in special units, killing and maiming civilians. There were those who had been victims of these terrors and carried fresh scars to show for it. So whenever people saw us, we reminded them of the massacres, and that struck fear in their hearts again. Some people tried to hurt us to protect themselves, their families and communities. Because of these things, we decided to bypass villages by walking through the nearby bushes. This way we would be safe and avoid causing chaos. This was one of the consequences of the civil war. People stopped trusting each other, and every stranger became an enemy. Even people who knew you became extremely careful about how they related or spoke to you.

One day, as soon as we had left the forested area of a village we had bypassed, a group of huge, muscular men sprang from the bushes onto the path in front of us. Raising their machetes and hunting rifles, they ordered us to stop. The men were the voluntary guards of their village and had been asked by their chief to bring us back.

A large crowd had gathered in the chief's compound for our arrival. The huge men pushed us to the ground in front of them and tied our feet with strong ropes. Then our hands were pulled behind our backs until our elbows touched, making our chests tight from the pressure. I was in tears from the pain. I tried to roll on my back, but that made it even worse.

"Are you rebels or spies?" The chief stamped his staff on the ground.

"No." Our voices trembled.

The chief became very angry. "If you do not tell me the truth, I am going to have these men tie stones to your bodies and throw you in the river," he roared.

We told him we were students and this was a big misunderstanding.

The crowd shouted, "Drown the rebels."

The guards walked into the circle and started searching our pockets. One of them found a rap cassette in my pocket and handed it to the chief. He asked for it to be played.

You down with OPP (Yeah you know me)
You down with OPP (Yeah you know me)
You down with OPP (Yeah you know me)
Who's down with OPP (Every last homie)

The chief stopped the music. He stroked his beard, thinking.

"Tell me," he said, turning to me, "how did you get this foreign music?"

I told him that we rapped. He didn't know what rap music was, so I did my best to explain it to him. "It is similar to telling parables, but in the white man's language," I concluded. I also told him that we were dancers and had a group in Mattru Jong, where we used to attend school.

"Mattru Jong?" he asked, and called for a young man who was from that village. The boy was brought before the chief and asked if he knew us and if he had ever heard us speak parables in the white man's language. He knew my name, my brother's, and those of my friends. He remembered us from performances we had done. None of us knew him, not even by his face, but we warmly smiled as if we recognized him as well. He saved our lives.

We were untied and treated to some cassava and smoked fish. We ate, thanked the villagers, and got ready to move on. The chief and some of the men who had tied our hands and feet offered us a place to stay in the village. We thanked them for their generosity and left. We knew that the rebels would eventually reach the village.

Slowly, we walked on a path through a thick forest. The trees hesitantly swayed with the quiet wind. The sky looked as if it was filled with smoke, endless gray smoke that made the sun dull. Around sunset we arrived at an abandoned village with six mud houses. We sat on the floor of the verandah of one of the houses. I looked at Junior, whose face was sweating. He had been so quiet lately. He looked at me and smiled a little before his face resumed its dullness. He got up and walked out to the yard. Never moving, he stared at the sky until the sun disappeared. On his way back to sit on the verandah, he picked up a stone and played with it throughout the evening. I kept looking at him, hoping that we could have another eye contact and maybe he would then say something about what was going on in his head. But he wouldn't look up. He only played with the stone in his hand and stared at the ground.

Once, Junior taught me how to skip a stone on a river. We had gone to fetch water and he told me he had learned a new magic that let him make stones walk on water. Bending his body sideways, he threw stones out, and each one walked on the water farther than the last. He told me to try, but I couldn't do it. He promised to teach me the magic some other time. As we were walking back home with buckets of water on our heads, I slipped and fell, spilling the water. Junior gave me his bucket, took my empty one, and returned to the river. When he came home, the first thing he did was ask me if I was hurt from falling. I told him I was fine, but he examined my knees and elbows anyway, and when he was done, he tickled me. As I looked at him that evening

sitting on the verandah of a house in an unknown village, I wanted
him to ask me if I was fine.

Gibrilla, Talloi, Kaloko, and Khalilou were all looking at the top of
the forest that engulfed the village. Gibrilla's nose twitched as he sat
with his chin on his knee. When he exhaled, his whole body moved.
Talloi continuously tapped his foot on the floor, as if trying to distract
himself from thinking about the present. Kaloko was restless. He
couldn't sit still and kept switching positions, and sighed each time he
did so. Khalilou sat quietly. His face showed no emotion and his spirit
seemed to have wandered away from his body. I wanted to know how
Junior was feeling, but I couldn't find the right moment to break into
the silence of that evening. I wish I had.

The following morning, a large group of people passed through the
village. Among the travelers was a woman who knew Gibrilla. She told
him that his aunt was in a village about thirty miles from where we
were. She gave us directions. We filled our pockets with unripe oranges
that were sour and unbearable to eat but the only source of food at our
disposal, and we were on our way.

Kamator was very far away from Mattru Jong, where the rebels were
still in control, but the villagers were on guard and ready to move anytime. In return for food and a place to sleep, the six of us were appointed watchmen. Three miles from the village was a big hill. From
the top, one could see as far as a mile down the path toward the village.
It was at the top of that hill that we stood watch from early in the
morning until nightfall. We did this for about a month and nothing
happened. Still, we knew the rebels well enough to brace for their arrival. But we lost our vigilance to the gradual passing of time.

The season for planting was approaching. The first rain had fallen,
softening the soil. Birds began building their nests in the mango trees.
Dew came down every morning and left the leaves wet and soaked the
soil. The odor of the soaked soil was irresistibly sharp at midday. It
made me want to roll on the ground. One of my uncles used to joke

that he would like to die at this time of year. The sun rose earlier than usual and was at its brightest in the blue, almost cloudless sky. The grass on the side of the path was half dry and half green. Ants could be seen on the ground carrying food into their holes. Even though we tried to convince them otherwise, the villagers grew certain the rebels weren't coming, and so they ordered us from our scouting posts and out into the fields. It wasn't easy.

I had always been a spectator of the art of farming and as a result never realized how difficult it was until those few months of my life, in 1993, when I had to assist in farming in the village of Kamator. The village inhabitants were all farmers, so I had no way to escape this fate.

Before the war, when I visited my grandmother during harvest season, the only thing she let me do was pour wine on the soil around the farm before harvest commenced, as part of a ceremony to thank the ancestors and the gods for providing fertile soil, healthy rice, and a successful farming year.

The first task we were given was to clear a massive plot of land the size of a football field. When we went to look at the bush that was supposed to be cut, I knew tough days lay ahead. The bush was thick and there were lots of palm trees, each surrounded by trees that had woven their branches together. It was difficult to get around them and chop them down. The ground was covered with decayed leaves that had changed the top color of the brown soil to dark. Termites could be heard rummaging under the rotten leaves. Every day we would repeatedly stoop and stand under the bushes, swinging machetes and axes at the trees and palms that had to be cut lower to the ground so that they wouldn't grow fast again and disrupt the crop that was to be planted. Sometimes when we swung the machetes and axes, their weight would send us flying into the bushes, where we would lie for a bit and rub our aching shoulders. Gibrilla's uncle would shake his head and say, "You lazy town boys."

On the first morning of clearing, Gibrilla's uncle assigned each of us a portion of the bush to be cut down. We spent three days cutting down our portions. He was done in less than three hours.

When I held the cutlass in my hand to start attacking the bush, Gibrilla's uncle couldn't help himself. He burst out laughing before he showed me how to hold the cutlass properly. I spent restless minutes swinging the cutlass with all my might at trees that he would cut with one strike.

The first two weeks were extremely painful. I suffered from back pains and muscle aches. Worst of all, the flesh on the palms of my hands was peeled, swollen, and blistered. My hands were not used to holding a machete or an ax. After the clearing was done, the bush was left to dry. Later, when the cut bush was dried, we set fire to it and watched the thick smoke rise to the blue summer sky.

Next we had to plant cassava. To do this, we dug mini-holes in the ground using hoes. To take a break from this task, which required us to bend our upper bodies toward the ground for hours, we fetched cassava stalks, cut them into shorter pieces, and placed them in the holes. The only sounds we heard as we worked were the humming of tunes by expert farmers, the occasional flapping of a bird, the snaps of tree branches breaking in the nearby forest, and hellos from neighbors traveling the path either to their own farms or back to the village. At the end of the day, I sometimes would sit on a log at the village square and watch the younger boys play their wrestling games. One of the boys, about seven, always started a fight, and his mother would pull him away by his ear. I saw myself in him. I was a troublesome boy as well and always got into fights in school and at the river. Sometimes I stoned kids I couldn't beat up. Since we didn't have a mother at home, Junior and I were the misfits in our community. The separation of our parents left marks on us that were visible to the youngest child in our town. We became the evening gossip.

"Those poor boys," some would say.

"They aren't going to have any good complete training," others would worriedly remark as we walked by.

I was so angry at the way they pitied us that I would sometimes kick their children's behinds at school, especially those who gave us the look that said, My parents talk about you a lot.

We farmed for three months at Kamator and I never got used to it. The only times that I enjoyed were the afternoon breaks, when we went swimming in the river. There, I would sit on the clear sandy bottom of the river and let the current take me downstream, where I would resurface, put on my dirty clothes, and return to the farm. The sad thing about all that hard labor was that, in the end, it all went to ruin, because the rebels did eventually come and everyone ran away, leaving their farms to be covered by weeds and devoured by animals.

It was during that attack in the village of Kamator that my friends and I separated. It was the last time I saw Junior, my older brother.

7

THE ATTACK HAPPENED unexpectedly one night. There hadn't even been any rumors that the rebels were as close as fifty miles from Kamator. They just walked into the village from out of nowhere.

It was about 8:00 p.m., when people were performing the last prayer of the day. The imam was oblivious to what was going on until it was too late. He stood in front of everyone, facing east, vigorously reciting a long sura, and once prayer had started, no one was allowed to say anything that was not related to the performance of the prayer. I didn't go to the mosque that night, but Kaloko did. He said that upon realizing that the rebels were in the village, everyone quickly and silently left the mosque, one at a time, leaving the imam by himself as he stood there leading the prayer. Some people tried to whisper to him, but he ignored them. The rebels captured him and demanded to know what parts of the forest people were hiding in, but the imam refused to tell them. They bound his hands and feet with wire, tied him to an iron post, and set fire to his body. They didn't burn him completely, but the fire killed him. His semi-burnt remains were left in the village square. Kaloko said he saw this from the nearby bush where he hid.

During the attack, Junior was in the verandah room where all five of us slept. I was outside, sitting on the steps. I had no time to go look for him, since the attack was sudden, but instead had to run into the bush alone. That night I slept by myself, leaning on a tree. In the morning I found Kaloko, and together we returned to the village. The semi-burnt body of the imam, as Kaloko had described it, was there in the village square. I could see the pain he had felt by looking at the way his teeth were bared. All the houses were burned. There wasn't a sign of life anywhere. We looked in the thick forest for Junior and our friends, but they weren't anywhere to be found. We stumbled across a family we knew and they let us hide with them in the bush by the swamp. We stayed with them for two weeks, two weeks that felt like months. Each day went by very slowly as I busied myself thinking about what other possibilities lay ahead. Was there an end to this madness, and was there any future for me beyond the bushes? I thought about Junior, Gibrilla, Talloi, and Khalilou. Had they been able to escape the attack? I was losing everyone, my family, my friends. I remembered when my family moved to Mogbwemo. My father held a ceremony to bless our new home. He invited our new neighbors, and my father stood up during the ceremony and said, "I pray to the gods and ancestors that my family will always be together." He looked at us, my mother held my little brother, and Junior and I stood next to each other with toffee in our mouths.

One of the elders stood up and added to what my father had said: "I pray to the gods and ancestors that your family will always be together, even when one of you crosses into the spirit world. To family and community." The old man raised his open hands in the air. My father came over and stood by my mother and motioned for Junior and me to come closer. We did, and my father put his arms around us. The gathering clapped and a photographer took a few snapshots.

I pressed my fingers on my eyelids to hold back my tears and wished that I could have my family together again.

Once every three days we visited Kamator to see if people had returned, but each visit was in vain, as there wasn't a sign of a living thing. The silence in the village was too scary. I was scared when the wind blew, shaking the thatched roofs, and I felt as if I were out of my body wandering somewhere. There weren't footprints of any kind. Not even a lizard dared to crawl through the village. The birds and crickets didn't sing. I could hear my footsteps louder than my heartbeat. During these visits, we brought with us brooms so that we could sweep away our footprints as we went back to our hiding place to avoid being followed. The last time Kaloko and I visited the village, dogs were feasting on the burnt remains of the imam. One dog had his arm and the other his leg. Above, vultures circled, preparing to descend on the body as well.

I became frustrated with living in fear. I felt as if I was always waiting for death to come to me, so I decided to go somewhere where at least there was some peace. Kaloko was afraid to leave. He thought that by leaving the bush we would be walking toward death. He decided to stay in the swamp.

I had nothing to carry, so I filled my pockets with oranges, tied the laces of my tattered *crapes*, and I was ready to go. I said goodbye to everyone and headed west. As soon as I left the hiding area and was on the path, I felt as if I was being wrapped in a blanket of sorrow. It came over me instantly. I started to cry. I didn't know why. Maybe it was because I was afraid of what might lie ahead. I sat on the side of the path for a while until my tears were gone, and then moved on.

I walked all day and didn't run into a single person on the path or in the villages that I passed through. There were no footprints to be seen, and the only sounds I heard were those of my breathing and my footsteps.

For five days, I walked from dawn to dusk, never coming in contact with any human being. At night I slept in abandoned villages. Every morning I made my own fate by deciding which way I was going to go. My goal was to avoid walking in the direction from where I had come. I ran out of oranges on the first day, but I collected more at every village that I slept in. Sometimes I would come across cassava farms. I would uproot some and eat them raw. The other food that was available in most villages was coconut. I didn't know how to climb a coconut tree. I had tried, but it was just impossible, until one day when I was very hungry and thirsty. I arrived at a village where there was nothing to eat except for the coconuts that sloppily hung from the trees, as if teasing me, daring me to pluck them. It is difficult to explain how it happened, but I mounted the coconut tree quite fast and unexpectedly. By the time I realized what I was doing and thought about my inexperience in this particular art, I was already at the top of the branches and plucking coconuts. I climbed down just as quickly and looked around for something to crack them with. Luckily, I found an old machete and got to work on the coconut shells. After I was done snacking, I found myself a hammock and rested for a while.

I got up well rested and thought, I think I have enough energy now to climb and pick more coconuts for the road. But it was impossible. I couldn't even climb past the middle of the trunk. I tried again and again, but each attempt was more pitiful than the last. I hadn't laughed for a long time, but this made me laugh uncontrollably. I could have written a science paper on the experience.

On the sixth day, I came in contact with humans. I had just left the village that I slept in the previous night and was on my way to look for another one when I heard voices ahead of me, rising and fading as the wind changed direction. I got off the path and walked carefully, minding my footstep on dried leaves in the forest to avoid making any sound. I stood behind the bushes, watching the people I had heard. There were eight of them down at the river, four young boys about twelve years old—my age—two girls, a man, and a woman. They were swimming. After observing for a while and determining that they were harmless, I decided to go down to the river for a swim as well. In order to avoid scaring them, I walked back to the path and headed toward them.

The man was the first to see me. "Kushe-oo. How de body, sir?" I greeted him. His eyes searched my smiling face. He didn't say anything and I thought maybe he didn't speak Krio. So I said hello in Mende, my tribal language.

"*Bu-wah. Bi ga huin ye na.*" He still didn't respond. I took my clothes off and dived into the river. When I rose to the surface, all of them had stopped swimming but remained in the water. The man, who must have been the father, asked me, "Where are you from and where are you going?" He was Mende and he understood Krio very well.

"I am from Mattru Jong and I have no idea where I am going." I wiped the water off my face and then continued, "Where are you and your family headed?" He ignored my question by pretending he didn't hear me. I proceeded to ask him if he knew the fastest way to Bonthe, an island in the south of Sierra Leone and one of the safest places at that time, according to hearsay. He told me that if I kept walking toward the sea, I would eventually find people who might have a better understanding about how to get to Bonthe. It was clear from the tone of his voice that he didn't want me around and didn't trust me. I looked at the curious and skeptical faces of the children and the woman. I was glad to see other faces and at the same time disappointed that the war had destroyed the enjoyment of the very experience of meeting people. Even a twelve-year-old couldn't be trusted anymore. I got out of the water, thanked the man, and was on my way, heading in the direction he had pointed that led toward the sea.

Sadly, I do not know the names of most of the villages that sheltered and provided me food during those times. No one was there to ask, and in those parts of the country there weren't any signs that said the name of this or that village.

8

I WALKED for two days straight without sleeping. I stopped only at streams to drink water. I felt as if somebody was after me. Often, my shadow would scare me and cause me to run for miles. Everything felt awkwardly brutal. Even the air seemed to want to attack me and break my neck. I knew I was hungry, but I didn't have the appetite to eat or the strength to find food. I had passed through burnt villages where dead bodies of men, women, and children of all ages were scattered like leaves on the ground after a storm. Their eyes still showed fear, as if death hadn't freed them from the madness that continued to unfold. I had seen heads cut off by machetes, smashed by cement bricks, and rivers filled with so much blood that the water had ceased flowing. Each time my mind replayed these scenes, I increased my pace. Sometimes I closed my eyes hard to avoid thinking, but the eye of my mind refused to be closed and continued to plague me with images. My body twitched with fear, and I became dizzy. I could see the leaves on the trees swaying, but I couldn't feel the wind.

On the third day, I found myself in the middle of a thick forest, standing beneath huge trees whose leaves and branches made it difficult to see the sky. I didn't remember how I had gotten there. Night was approaching, so I found a suitable tree that wasn't too high to climb; it had weaved branches with another to form something like a hammock. I spent the night in the arms of those trees, between earth and sky.

The next morning I was determined to find my way out of the forest, even though my back ached painfully from sleeping in the trees. On my way, I came to a spring that ran from under a gigantic rock. I sat by it to rest, and there I had eye contact with a huge dark snake that retreated behind the bush. I found a long strong stick to protect myself as I sat playing with leaves on the ground to avoid bringing up thoughts that occupied my mind. But my mind continued to torment me, and every effort to clear away the terrible thoughts was in vain. So I decided to walk, tapping the ground with the stick I held. I walked all morning and into the evening, but in the end found myself at the same place where I had slept the previous night. That was when I finally came to accept that I was lost and it was going to take a while to get out of where I was. I decided to make my new home a little bit more comfortable by adding leaves to the weaved branches to make them less hard to sleep on.

I walked around to familiarize myself with my vicinity. As I was getting acquainted with my new home, I cleared the dried leaves. Then I took a stick and drew lines on the ground from my sleeping place to the spring where I had met my new neighbor, the snake. There was another one drinking water and it became motionless upon seeing me. As I went about my business, I heard it crawling away. I drew lines by parting the dried leaves on the ground. These lines helped me from getting lost in between the spring and my sleeping place. After I finished familiarizing myself with the area, I sat down and tried to think about how I was going to get out of the forest. But that didn't go well, since I was afraid of thinking. I eventually decided that maybe it was better to be where I was. Even though I was lost and lonely, it was safe for the time being.

Along the spring there were several trees with a ripe fruit that I had never seen. Birds came to eat this strange fruit every morning. I decided to try some of it, since it was the only edible thing around. It was either take the chance and eat this fruit that might poison me or die of hunger. I decided to eat the fruit. I thought if the birds ate it and lived, maybe I could, too. The fruit was shaped like a lemon, with an outer layer of mixed colors of yellow and red. Inside was a crusty, watery, fruity part with a very tiny seed. It smelled like a mixture of ripe mango, orange, and something else that was irresistibly inviting. Hesitantly, I plucked one and took a bite. It didn't taste as good as it smelled, but it was satisfying. I must have had about twelve of them. Afterward, I drank some water and sat waiting for the result.

I thought about when Junior and I had visited Kabati and would take walks with our grandfather on paths around the coffee farms by the village. He would point out medicinal leaves and trees whose barks were important medicines. During each visit, Grandfather always gave us a special medicine that was supposed to enhance the brain's capacity to absorb and retain knowledge. He made this medicine by writing a special Arabic prayer on a *waleh* (slate) with ink that was made of another medicine. The writing was then washed off the slate, and that water, which they called *Nessie*, was put in a bottle. We took it with us and were supposed to keep it a secret and drink it before we studied for exams. This medicine worked. During my primary-school years and part of my secondary-school years, I was able to permanently retain everything that I learned. Sometimes it worked so well that during examinations I could visualize my notes and all that was written on each page of my textbooks. It was as if the books had been imprinted inside my head. This wonder was one of many in my childhood. To this day, I have an excellent photographic memory that enables me to remember details of the day-to-day moments of my life, indelibly.

I looked around the forest for one of the medicinal leaves that Grandfather had said remove poison from the body. I might need it if the fruit I had eaten was poisonous. But I couldn't find the plant.

Nothing happened after a couple of hours, so I decided to take a bath. I hadn't had time to take one for a while. My clothes were dirty, my *crapes* were rotten, and my body was sticky with dirt. When I first threw water on my skin, it became slimy. There was no soap, but in the forest there was an area that had a particular kind of grass that could be used as a substitute. I had learned about this grass during one of the summers when I visited my grandmother. When I squeezed a bunch of the grasses together, they provided foam that left my body with a fresh scent. After I had finished taking a bath, I washed my clothes or, rather, soaked and spread them on the grass to dry. I sat naked, cleaning my teeth with sapwood. A deer came by and watched me suspiciously before it went about its affairs. I resisted thinking by listening to the sound of the forest as songs of birds collided with the shouting of monkeys and the cackle of baboons.

By evening, my clothes were still damp, so I put them on so that the heat of my body would dry them faster before night fell. I was still alive, despite eating the nameless fruit, so I ate some more for dinner. The following morning, I ate some more for breakfast and later for lunch and dinner again. The nameless fruit became my only source of food. The fruit was plentiful, but I knew that sooner or later there would be no more. Sometimes I felt as if the birds gave me angry looks for eating so much of their food.

The most difficult part of being in the forest was the loneliness. It became unbearable each day. One thing about being lonesome is that you think too much, especially when there isn't much else you can do. I didn't like this and I tried to stop myself from thinking, but nothing seemed to work. I decided to just ignore every thought that came to my head, because it brought too much sadness. Apart from eating and drinking water and once every other day taking a bath, I spent most of my time fighting myself mentally in order to avoid thinking about what I had seen or wondering where my life was going, where my family and friends were. The more I resisted thinking, the longer the days became, and I felt as if my head was becoming heavier each passing day. I became restless and was afraid to sleep for fear that my suppressed thoughts would appear in my dreams.

As I searched the forest for more food and to find a way out, I feared coming in contact with wild animals like leopards, lions, and wild pigs. So I stayed closer to trees that I could easily mount to hide myself from these animals. I walked as fast as I could, but the more I walked, the more it seemed I was getting deeper into the thickness of the forest. The harder I tried to get out, the bigger and taller the trees became. This was a problem, because it got difficult to find a tree that was easy to climb and had suitable branches to sleep in.

One evening, as I searched for a tree with a forked branch to sleep in, I heard grunts. I wasn't exactly sure what animals were producing such noisy grunts, but they became louder. I climbed a tree to be safe. As I sat there, a herd of wild pigs came running. It was the first time I had seen wild pigs and they were huge, all of them. If they stood up, they would all be taller than me. Each had forked teeth extending out of its mouth. As they passed underneath me, one of the biggest pigs stopped and sniffed the air in all directions. It must have sensed my presence. When they were gone, I climbed down, and all of a sudden a couple of enormous pigs came running at me. They chased me for about half a mile as I looked for a tree to climb. Fortunately, I found one that I was able to mount in one jump. The pigs stopped and started charging at the bottom of the tree. They grunted loudly and the rest of the herd came back. They all started charging at the tree and tried to chew the bottom. I climbed higher and higher. After a while they finally gave up as a cricket started calling for night to commence.

My grandmother once told me a story about a notorious hunter of wild pigs who used magic to transform himself into a wild boar. He would then lead the herd into an open area of the forest where he would change back into human form, then trap and shoot the pigs. One day during his trickery, a small pig saw the hunter biting a plant that enabled him to return to his human form. The pig told all its companions what it had seen. The herd searched the forest for the hunter's magic plant and destroyed every single one of them. The next day the hunter performed his trickery and lured the herd into an open-

Hope

ing. But he couldn't find the plant to become human again. The pigs tore him to pieces. Since that day, the wild pigs have distrusted all humans, and whenever they see a person in the forest, they think he or she is there to avenge the hunter.

After the pigs had gone and I had surveyed the terrain to my satisfaction, I climbed down and continued walking. I wanted to be away from that area before dawn, since I feared that if I stayed I might run into the wild pigs again. I walked all night and continued during the day. At the beginning of night, I saw owls coming from their hiding places, revolving their eyes, and stretching to become familiar with their surroundings and get ready for the night. I was walking very fast but very quietly, until I accidentally stepped on the tail of a snake. It started hissing and scuttling toward me. I ran as fast as I could for a long time. When I was six, my grandfather had inserted a medicine into my skin that protected me from snakebite and enabled me to control snakes. But as soon as I started school, I began to doubt the power of the medicine. After that, I was no longer able to make snakes stop in their tracks until I went by.

When I was very little, my father used to say, "If you are alive, there is hope for a better day and something good to happen. If there is nothing good left in the destiny of a person, he or she will die." I thought about these words during my journey, and they kept me moving even when I didn't know where I was going. Those words became the vehicle that drove my spirit forward and made it stay alive.

I had spent more than a month in the forest when I finally ran into people again. The only living things I had met were monkeys, snakes, wild pigs, and deer, none of which I could have a conversation with. Sometimes I watched the little monkeys practice jumping from tree to tree or watched the curious eyes of a deer that sensed my presence. The sounds of branches snapping off trees became my music. There were certain days when the sounds of the branches breaking made a consistent rhythm that I would enjoy very much, and the sonority of it would echo for a while and would gradually fade into the depths of the forest.

I was walking slowly, staggering from hunger, back pain, and fatigue, when I ran into some young people my age at an intersection where two paths merged into one. I was wearing a pair of trousers I had recently found hanging on a pole in an abandoned village. They were extremely big for me, so I had tied them with ropes so they wouldn't fall off while I walked. We all arrived at the junction at the same time, and upon seeing each other, we became paralyzed with fear. As I stood there, unable to run, I recognized a few of the faces and I smiled to break the tension and uncertainty. There were six boys, and three of them, Alhaji, Musa, and Kanei, had attended Centennial Secondary School with me in Mattru Jong. They weren't close friends, but the four of us had been flogged once for talking back to the senior prefect. We had nodded at one another after that punishment, which we all agreed was unnecessary. I shook hands with the boys.

I could tell who was from what tribe by the marks on their cheeks and their features. Alhaji and Saidu were Temne, and Kanei, Jumah, Musa, and Moriba were Mende. They told me they were heading for a village called Yele in Bonthe district that they had heard was safe because it was occupied by the Sierra Leone Armed Forces.

Quietly I followed them as I tried to remember all their names, especially the names of the faces I recognized among them. I walked in the back, creating a little distance between us. I began to realize how uncomfortable I felt being around people. Kanei, who was older, perhaps sixteen, asked me where I'd been. I smiled without answering. He tapped me on the shoulder as if he knew what I had experienced. "Circumstances will change and things will be fine, just hold on a little more," he said, tapping my shoulder again and nodding. I responded with a smile.

Once again I was with a group of boys. This time there were seven of us. I knew this was going to be a problem, but I didn't want to be by myself anymore. Our innocence had been replaced by fear and we had become monsters. There was nothing we could do about it. Sometimes we ran after people shouting that we were not what they thought, but this made them more scared. We hoped to ask people for directions. It was impossible.

We had traveled for more than six days when we came in contact with a very old man who could barely walk. He sat on the verandah of a house in the middle of the village. His face was too wrinkled to still be alive, yet his dark skin was shiny and he spoke slowly, gobbling the words in his jaws before he let them out. As he spoke, the veins on his forehead became visible through his skin.

"Everyone ran when they heard of the 'seven boys' on their way here. I couldn't run at all. So they left me behind. No one was willing to carry me and I didn't want to be a burden," he said.

We explained to him where we were from and where we wanted to go. He asked us to stay for a while and keep him company.

"You young fellows must be hungry. There are some yams in that hut over there. Can you boys cook some for me and yourselves?" he politely asked. When we were almost finished eating the yams, he said slowly, "My children, this country has lost its good heart. People don't trust each other anymore. Years ago, you would have been heartily welcomed in this village. I hope that you boys can find safety before this untrustworthiness and fear cause someone to harm you."

He drew a map on the ground with his walking stick. "This is how you get to Yele," he said.

"What is your name?" Kanei asked the old man.

He smiled as if he knew that one of us would ask this question. "There is no need to know my name. Just refer to me as the old man who got left behind when you get to the next village." He looked at all our faces and spoke softly, with no sadness in his voice.

"I will not be alive to see the end of this war. So, to save a place in your memories for other things, I won't tell you my name. If you survive this war, just remember me as the old man you met. You boys should be on your way." He pointed his staff toward the path that lay ahead of us. As we walked away, he erased the map with his foot and waved us off with a raised right hand and a nod. Before the village disappeared from our sight, I turned around to take one last look at the old man. His head was down and he had both hands on his staff. It was clear to me that he knew his days would soon be over, and he didn't bother to be afraid for himself. But he was for us.

Someone had started a rumor about the "seven boys," us. Many times during our journey we were surrounded by muscular men with machetes who almost killed us before they realized that we were just children running away from the war. Sometimes I looked at the blades of the machetes and thought about how much it would hurt to be chopped with one. Other times I was so hungry and tired that I didn't care. At crowded villages where we sometimes stopped to spend the night, the men stayed up to keep an eye on us. When we went to the river to wash our faces, mothers would grab their children and run home.

9

ONE MORNING, immediately after we had passed a deserted village, we started hearing something like the roar of big engines, the rolling of metal drums on a tar road, a thunder exploding, roll after roll. All these sounds reached our ears simultaneously. We hurriedly deviated from the path, running into the bushes and lying on the ground. We searched one another's faces for an explanation of this strange sound. Even Kanei, who sometimes had answers, couldn't tell us what we were hearing. We all looked at him and his face contorted with confusion.

"We have to find out what it is or we can't continue on to Yele," Kanei whispered, and then began to crawl toward the sound. We followed him, quietly dragging our bodies on rotten leaves. As we got closer, the sound intensified and a heavy breeze shook the trees above us. We could clearly see the blue sky, but nothing else. Kanei hesitantly sat on his heels and surveyed the area.

"It is just water, lots of it, and sand, lots of it." Kanei was still looking.

"What is making the noise, then?" Alhaji asked.

"All I am looking at is water and sand," Kanei replied, and then waved us to come closer and take a look. We sat on our heels for a while, looking in different directions, trying to locate what was making the sound. Without saying anything to us, Kanei crawled out of the bushes and started walking on the sand, toward the water.

It was the Atlantic Ocean. The sounds we had heard were those of the waves hitting the shore. I had seen parts of the ocean but had never stood at the shore of one this vast. It spread out beyond the vision of my eyes. The sky was at its bluest and seemed to curve down and join with the ocean in the distance. My eyes widened, a smile forming on my face. Even in the middle of the madness there remained that true and natural beauty, and it took my mind away from my current situation as I marveled at this sight.

We walked closer and sat at the edge of the sand and stared at the ocean, admiring the display of the waves in succession. They came in three folds. The first was small but powerful enough to break a person's leg. The second was high and more powerful than the first, and the third was a spectacle. It rolled and rose higher than the shoreline as it moved forward. We ran away from where we sat. The wave hit the shore so hard that it sent sand particles flying high up in the sky. When we went back to look, the waves had thrown out unwanted flotsam from the ocean, including some big crabs that I guess weren't strong enough to cling to the ocean floor, but they were still alive.

It was a calm walk along the sand, since we didn't expect trouble in this part of the country. We chased and wrestled each other in the sand, played somersault and running games. We even bundled up Alhaji's old shirt and tied a rope around it to make a soccer ball. We then played a game, and each time one of us scored a goal, he would celebrate with a *soukous* dance. We shouted, laughed, and sang our secondary-school songs.

We started walking on the sandy beach early in the morning and saw the sunrise. At midday we saw a cluster of huts ahead and raced each other toward them. When we arrived there, we suddenly became worried. There was no one in the village. Mortars lay in the sand, rice spilling out of them; jerry cans leaked water, and fires were left unattended under cooking huts. Our first guess was that the rebels might have been there. Before we could think of anything else, fishermen sprang from behind huts with machetes, fishing spears, and nets in their hands. We were so shocked by this sudden uproar that none of us was able to run. Instead, we shouted, "Please, we are harmless and just passing by," in every possible one of the eighteen local languages that each of us knew. The fishermen jabbed us with the flat edges of their weapons until we fell on the ground. They sat on top of us, tied our hands, and took us to their chief.

The villagers had heard a rumor that some young people, believed to be rebels, were heading their way. Upon hearing this, they had armed themselves and hid, waiting to defend their homes and protect their families. This should not have been a big shock to us, but we didn't expect it to happen here, since we thought we were now far from harm. They asked us several questions along the lines of where were we from? where were we going? and why did we choose that direction? Alhaji, the tallest among us and sometimes mistaken for the oldest, tried to explain to the chief that we were just passing by. Afterward, the men yanked our torn *crapes* off our feet, untied us, and chased us out of their village, waving their spears and machetes, and screaming after us.

We didn't realize what sort of punishment the fishermen had given us until we stopped running away from their village. The sun was in the middle of the sky, it was over 120 degrees, and we were barefoot. The humidity by the sea was less than inland, but since there were no trees to provide shade, the sun penetrated right into the sand, making it hot and loose. Walking barefoot on the sand was like walking on a hot tar road. The only escape from this pain was to keep walking and hope for something miraculous. We couldn't walk in the water or the wet sand near its edge. It was very deep between where we walked and where the water met the land, and the waves were dangerous. After I had cried for several hours, my feet became numb. I continued walking but couldn't feel the soles of my feet.

We walked on the hot, burning sand until sunset. I have never longed for a day to conclude as I did that day. I thought the arrival of sunset would heal my pain. But as the heat died down, the anesthesia also wore away. Each time I lifted my feet, the veins in them tightened and I felt the sand particles digging into my bleeding soles. The next several miles were so long that I didn't think I would be able to make it. I perspired and my body shuddered from the pain. Finally, we came upon a hut that was on the sand. None of us was able to talk. We walked inside and sat down on logs around a fireplace. There were tears in my eyes, but I was unable to cry because I was too thirsty to make a sound. I looked around to see the faces of my traveling companions. They were crying as well, without a sound. Hesitantly, I looked under my feet. Peeled flesh hung down and congealed blocks of blood and particles of sand clung to each hanging bit of skin. It looked as if someone had literally used a blade to cut the flesh under my feet from the heel to the toes. Discouraged, I looked into the sky through a tiny hole in the thatched roof, trying not to think about my feet. As we sat in silence, the man whose hut we had occupied came in. He stopped at the door, and was about to turn around when he noticed our suffering. His eyes met our frightened faces. Musa had just lifted his foot and was trying to separate the sand from his flesh. The rest of us were holding our knees so that our feet wouldn't touch the ground. The man motioned for Musa to stop what he was about to do. He shook his head and left.

A few minutes later, he returned, carrying a basket full of some type of grass. He quietly made a fire and heated the grasses and then placed them underneath each of our hanging feet. The steam from the grass rose to our soles, and it gradually lessened the pain. The man left without saying anything.

Later he returned with fried-fish soup, rice, and a bucket of water. He put the food before us and motioned for us to eat. Again he disappeared, returning a few minutes later, this time smiling widely. He had a fishing net on his shoulder and held a pair of oars and a big flashlight.

"You peekin dem dae feel betteh, right?" Without waiting to hear whether we were feeling better or not, he went on to tell us where the

sleeping mats were and that he was going fishing and would be back in the morning. He didn't even bother to ask our names. I guess he didn't think it was necessary or important at that moment. Before he left, he gave us ointment to rub on our feet and stressed that we do it before going to sleep. We were very quiet that night. No one said a word.

The following morning our nameless host came again with food and a smile on his face that said he was glad that we were doing fine. We couldn't walk well, so we just hobbled around the hut and made fun of each other to avoid boredom.

Kanei boasted about being an excellent soccer player. Musa threw him a groundnut shell; Kanei moved his foot to kick it, but then realized that it would hurt and abruptly swung his foot back, dragging it against a stone. He began to blow on his sole, in pain.

"What kind of soccer player are you going to be if you are afraid to kick an empty groundnut shell?" Musa laughed. We all gradually began to laugh.

Musa had a round face, and he was short and bulky, with tiny round ears that matched his face. His eyes were big and looked as if they wanted to leave his face. Whenever he wanted to convince us of something, they would brighten.

Kanei had a long and calm face, and unlike Musa he was skinny and had short, really dark hair that he took great care of every morning, or whenever we stopped at a river or a stream. He would rub water on his head and take his time to carefully arrange his hair. "Are you meeting a girl somewhere?" Alhaji would ask, giggling. Kanei, with his soft yet authoritative voice, always seemed to know what to say and how to handle certain situations better than the rest of us.

Whenever Alhaji spoke, he used elaborate gestures. It was as if he wanted his already long hands to extend toward whomever he was talking to. He and Jumah were friends. They walked next to each other. Jumah was always nodding his head, agreeing to whatever the lanky Alhaji said to him as we walked. Jumah used his head to gesture, rather than his hands. Whenever he spoke, he waved his head left to right. He kept his hands crossed behind his back most of the time, like an old man.

Saidu and Moriba were almost as quiet as I. They always sat next to each other, away from the group. Saidu breathed hard as we walked. His ears were large, and when he was listening, they stood up like a deer's. Moriba always told him that he must have extra hearing ability. Moriba mostly played with his hands, examining the lines on his palm and rubbing his fingers as he whispered to himself.

I barely spoke.

I knew Alhaji, Kanei, and Musa from my former secondary school. We never talked much about our past, especially our families. The few conversations we had that weren't related to our journey were mostly about soccer and school before we resumed our silence.

The pains we felt from our feet subsided on the fourth night. We went for a walk around the hut, and during our stroll I found out that the hut was only about half a mile from the main village; at night we could see smoke rising from the tiny village's cooking huts.

We stayed in the hut for a week. Our host brought us water and food every morning and night. He had the whitest teeth that I had ever seen, and he was shirtless all the time. Sometimes when he came to check on us in the morning, he had chewing sap in his mouth. I asked him one morning for his name. He laughed softly. "It is not necessary. This way we will all be safe."

The following night, our host decided to take us to a part of the Atlantic Ocean that was nearby. As we walked, he engaged us in conversation. We learned that he was Sherbro, one of the many tribes in Sierra Leone. When he heard the stories of how we had walked from Mattru Jong, he couldn't believe us. He said he had heard about the war but still had difficulty believing that people could do the things that he had heard they did. Our host had been born in the main village and never left. Traders came to his village with clothing items, rice, and other cooking ingredients to exchange for salt and fish, so he didn't need to go anywhere. If I had to guess, I would say he was in his early twenties. He said he was going to get married the next month and was looking forward to it. I asked why his hut was removed from the village. He explained that it was his fishing hut, where he kept his nets and other fishing items and where he dried fish during the rainy season.

When we got to the ocean, we walked to an inlet where the sea wasn't rough. We sat on the banks. "Put you foot nah de wahter, make de salt wahter soakam." He also said the salt water was good for healing the pain and preventing tetanus. Our host sat aside, looking at us, and each time I looked at him he was smiling and his white teeth stood out against his dark face. The dry breeze from inland coupled with the cool ocean air was perfectly soothing. I wanted to know his name so badly, but I restrained myself.

"You boys must come here every night to put your feet in the ocean. This way you will be healed in less than a week," he said.

He looked in the sky, where the stars were beginning to be covered by fast-moving clouds. "I have to go take care of my canoe. It will rain soon, so you must go back to the hut." He started running in the sand toward the main village.

"I wish I could be that man. He is just so happy and content with his life," Alhaji said.

"He is a very nice man, too. I really want to know his name," Kanei said softly.

"Yes, yes." We all agreed with Kanei and went wandering into our own thoughts, which were interrupted by a sudden burst of rain. We hadn't listened to our host and left when he'd told us to. We hastened to the hut. There, we sat around the fire to dry ourselves and eat dried fish.

We had been with our host for two weeks and were feeling better when very early one morning, an older woman came to the hut. She woke us and told us to leave immediately. She said she was the mother of our host and that the people in the village had found out about us and were on their way to capture us. From the way she spoke, I could tell that she had known about us all along. She brought with her dried fish and fresh water for us to take on our journey. We didn't have enough time to thank her and tell her to thank her son for his hospitality. But from what she said, it was clear that she knew we were thankful and she cared about our safety more than anything else.

"My children, you must hurry now, and my blessings are with you." Her voice was trembling with sadness, and she wiped her disconsolate face as she disappeared behind the hut and headed back to the main village.

We were not fast enough to escape the men who came for us. Twelve of them ran after the seven of us, wrestling us to the sand. They tied our hands.

In truth, realizing that I would eventually be caught, I had stopped running and offered my hands to be tied. The man chasing me was a little taken aback. He approached me with caution and motioned another man walking behind me with a stick and machete to pay attention. As the man tied my hands, we exchanged a glance that lasted a few seconds. I opened my eyes wide, trying to tell him that I was just a twelve-year-old boy. But something in his eyes told me that he didn't care for my safety but only for his and his village's.

The men walked us to their village and made us sit outside in the sand in front of their chief. I had been through this before, and wondered if it was a new experience for my present traveling companions. They were all heaving as they tried to hold back their cries. I began to worry, because last time I had found someone in the village who had gone to school with us and saved us. This time we were a long way from Mattru Jong. A long way gone.

Most of the men were shirtless, but the chief was elegantly dressed. He wore traditional cotton clothes with intricate designs on the collar made of yellow and brown thread, zigzagged vertically across his chest. His brown leather sandals looked new and he carried a staff with carvings of birds, canoes, all sorts of animals, and a lion's head on the handle. The chief examined us for a while, and when he caught my eye, I gave him half a smile, which he dismissed by spitting on the ground from the kola nut he chewed. His voice was hoarse.

"You children have become little devils, but you came to the wrong village." He used his staff to gesture instead of his hands. "Well, this is the end of the road for devils like you. Out there in the ocean, even you rascals cannot survive."

"Undress them," he commanded the men who had caught us. I was trembling with fear but unable to cry. Alhaji, who stammered with terror, tried to say something, but the chief kicked the side of the stool that he sat on and proclaimed, "I do not want to hear any word from a devil."

Our nameless host and his mother stood in the crowd. His mother squeezed his hand each time the chief called us devils or screamed at us. As I was being undressed, the rap cassettes fell out of my pockets and the man who undressed me picked them up and handed them to the chief. The chief looked closely at the faces on the covers of the cassette cases. He carefully examined the Naughty by Nature cassette cover over and over, looking at the militant stance and tough expression on the faces of the three guys standing on broken rocks with a lamppost in the background, puzzled by their poses. He demanded that a cassette player be brought. One of the men told the chief that the only way we could possess such foreign cassettes was either by having looted them or if we were mercenaries. The chief may have bought the man's first point, but he disregarded his second point, as it was utterly stupid.

"These boys are no mercenaries, look at them." The chief went back to inspecting the cassettes. I was a little glad that he had called us boys and refrained from the word "devil." But I was extremely uncomfortable sitting naked in the sand. It was not a pleasant experience. Just the thought of what was happening was enough to get me agitated. I fought hard mentally to let my face show the opposite of what I felt. The flesh on my face twitched as we waited for the chief to grant us life or death.

When the cassette player was brought, the chief put the cassette in and pressed "play."

> *OPP how can I explain it*
> *I'll take you frame by frame it*
> *To have y'all jumpin' shall we singin' it*
> *O is for Other P is for People scratchin' temple . . .*

Everyone listened attentively, raising their eyebrows and cocking their heads as they tried to understand what kind of music this was. The chief abruptly stopped the song. Some of the villagers leaned against their round mud huts and others sat on the ground or on mortars. The men rolled the legs of their taffeta pants, women adjusted their wrappers, and the children stared at us, their hands inside their pockets or in their runny noses.

"Stand him up and bring him here," the chief commanded.

When I was brought closer, he asked me where I had gotten this type of music and what was the point of having it. I explained to him that it was called rap music and that myself, my brother, and my friends—not the ones I was with—used to listen to it and perform the songs at talent shows. I could tell that he found this interesting, as his face was beginning to relax. He asked the men to untie me and give me my pants.

"Now you show me how you, your brother, and friends did it," the chief said.

I rewound the tape, mimed, and danced to "OPP" barefoot in the sand. I didn't enjoy it, and for the first time I found myself thinking about the words of the song, closely listening to the subtle instruments in the beat. I had never done such a thing before, because I knew the words by heart and felt the beat. I didn't feel it this time. As I hopped up and down, hunched and raising my arms and feet to the music, I thought about being thrown in the ocean, about how difficult it would be to know that death was inevitable. The wrinkles on the chief's forehead began to ease. He still didn't smile, but he gave a sigh that said I was just a child. At the end of the song, he rubbed his beard and said that he was impressed with my dancing and found the singing "interesting." He asked for the next cassette to be played. It was LL Cool J. I mimed the song "I Need Love."

> *When I'm alone in my room sometimes I stare at the wall*
> *and in the back of my mind I hear my conscience call*

The chief turned his head from side to side as if trying to understand what I was saying. I watched him to see if his face was going to change for the worse, but a look of amusement flickered on his face. He ordered that all my friends be untied and given back their clothes. The chief explained to everyone that there had been a misunderstanding and that we were only children looking for safety. He wanted to know if we had stayed in the hut of our own accord or if the owner knew about us. I told him that we had stayed there on our own and that we hadn't come in contact with anyone until that morning. The chief told us that he was letting us go, but that we had to leave the area immediately. He gave me back my cassettes and we were on our way. As we walked, we examined the rope marks on our wrists and laughed about what had happened to avoid crying.

10

ONE OF THE UNSETTLING THINGS about my journey, mentally, physically, and emotionally, was that I wasn't sure when or where it was going to end. I didn't know what I was going to do with my life. I felt that I was starting over and over again. I was always on the move, always going somewhere. While we walked, I sometimes lagged behind, thinking about these things. To survive each passing day was my goal in life. At villages where we managed to find some happiness by being treated to food or fresh water, I knew that it was temporary and that we were only passing through. So I couldn't bring myself to be completely happy. It was much easier to be sad than to go back and forth between emotions, and this gave me the determination I needed to keep moving. I was never disappointed, since I always expected the worst to happen. There were nights when I couldn't sleep but stared into the darkest night until my eyes could see clearly through it. I thought about where my family was and whether they were alive.

One night while I sat outside in a village square thinking about how far I had come and what might lie ahead, I looked into the sky and saw how the thick clouds kept trying to cover the moon, yet it would reappear again and again to shine all night long. In some way my journey was like that of the moon—although I had even more thick clouds coming my way to make my spirit dull. I remembered something that Saidu had said one evening after we had survived another attack by men with spears and axes. Jumah, Moriba, and Musa were asleep on the verandah we occupied. Alhaji, Kanei, Saidu, and I were awake and quietly listening to the night. Saidu's heavy breathing made our silence less unbearable. After a few hours had gone by, Saidu spoke in a very deep voice, as if someone were speaking through him. "How many more times do we have to come to terms with death before we find safety?" he asked.

He waited a few minutes, but the three of us didn't say anything. He continued: "Every time people come at us with the intention of killing us, I close my eyes and wait for death. Even though I am still alive, I feel like each time I accept death, part of me dies. Very soon I will completely die and all that will be left is my empty body walking with you. It will be quieter than I am." Saidu blew on the palms of his hands to warm them and lay on the floor. His heavy breathing intensified and I knew he had fallen asleep. Gradually, Kanei and then Alhaji fell asleep. I sat on a wooden bench against the wall and thought about Saidu's words. Tears formed in my eyes and my forehead became warm, thinking about what Saidu had said. I tried not to believe that I too was dying, slowly, on my way to find safety. The only time I was able to fall asleep that night was when the last morning breeze, the one containing the irresistible urge to sleep, saved me from my wandering mind.

Even though our journey was difficult, every once in a while we were able to do something that was normal and made us happy for a brief moment. One morning we arrived at a village where the men were getting ready to go hunting. They invited us to join them. At the end of the hunt, one of the older men shouted, pointing at us, "We are going to feast tonight, and the strangers are welcome to stay." The other men clapped and began walking on the path back to the village.

We walked behind them. They sang, carrying their nets and the animals—mostly porcupines and deer—that had been caught on their shoulders.

Upon our arrival at the village, the women and children clapped to welcome us. It was past midday. The sky was blue and the wind was beginning to pick up. Some of the men shared the meat among several households, and the rest was given to the women to be cooked for the feast. We hung about in the village and fetched water for the women who were preparing the food. Most of the men had returned to work the farms.

I walked around the village by myself and found a hammock on one of the verandahs. I lay in it, swinging slowly to get my thoughts in motion. I began to think about the times when I visited my grandmother and I would sleep in the hammock at the farm. I would wake up staring into her eyes as she played with my hair. She would tickle me and then hand me a cucumber to eat. Junior and I would sometimes fight for the hammock, and if he got it, I would trick him by loosening its ropes so that he would fall once he sat in it. This would discourage him, and he would go about the farm doing something else. My grandmother knew about my tricks and made fun of me, calling me *carseloi*, which means spider. In many Mende stories the spider is the character that tricks other animals to get what he wants, but his tricks always backfire on him.

As I was thinking about these things, I fell out of the hammock. I was too lazy to get up, so I sat on the ground and thought about my two brothers, my father, mother, and grandmother. I wished to be with them.

I put my hands behind my head and lay on my back, trying to hold on to the memories of my family. Their faces seemed to be far off somewhere in my mind, and to get to them I had to bring up painful memories. I longed for the gentle, dark, and shiny old hands of my grandmother; my mother's tight enclosed embrace, during the times I visited her, as if hiding and protecting me from something; my father's laughter when we played soccer together and when he sometimes chased me in the evening with a bowl of cold water to get me to take a shower; my older brother's arms around me when we walked to school and when he sometimes elbowed me to stop me from saying things I would regret; and my little brother, who looked exactly like me and would sometimes tell people that his name was Ishmael when he did something wrong. I had trouble conjuring up these thoughts, and when I finally ventured into these memories, I became so sad that the bones in my body started to ache. I went to the river, dove into the water, and sat at the bottom, but my thoughts followed me.

In the evening after everyone had returned to the village, the food was brought outside to the village square. It was divided among plates and seven people ate from each plate. After the meal, the villagers started playing drums, and we all joined hands and danced in circles under the moonlight. During an interval after several songs, one of the men announced that when the dancing had been exhausted, "whenever that will be," he jokingly said, "the strangers will tell us stories about where they are from." He lifted his hands and motioned for the drummers to continue. During the festivities I thought about the biggest celebration we used to have in my town at the end of the year. The women would sing about all the gossip, the dramas, the fights, and everything that had happened that year.

Would they be able to sing about all that will happen by the end of this war? I thought.

I also wondered a bit why the villagers were so kind to us, but I didn't dwell on these thoughts, because I wanted to enjoy myself. The dance never ended that night and we had to leave early the next day, so we left as most of the villagers slept. We carried with us a plastic gallon of water and some smoked meat we had been given, and the old people we passed, sitting on their verandahs, waiting to be warmed by the morning sun, waved and said, "May the spirit of the ancestors be with you, children."

When we were walking, I turned around to see the village one last time. It was yet to be born for that day. A cock crowed to dispatch the last remains of night and to mute the crickets that couldn't let go of the darkness of their own accord. The sun was slowly rising but had already begun casting shadows on the huts and houses. I could still hear the drums echoing in my head from the previous night, but I refused to be happy. When I turned away from the village, my traveling companions were dancing in the sand, mimicking some of the dances we had seen.

"Show us what you've got," they said, clapping and circling me. I couldn't refuse. I started gyrating my hips to their claps, and they joined me. We placed our hands on each other's shoulders and walked forward, dancing to sounds we made with our mouths. I was carrying the smoked meat in a small bag that I waved in the air to increase the speed at which we kicked our feet from side to side. We danced and laughed into the morning. But gradually we stopped. It was as if we all knew that we could be happy for only a brief moment. We weren't in a hurry, so we walked slowly and quietly after we stopped dancing. At the end of the day we had finished drinking the water we were carrying.

Around nightfall we arrived at a very peculiar village. I am in fact not sure if it was a village. There was one large house and one kitchen less than a kilometer from the house. The pots were moldy, and there was a small storage house. The place was located in the middle of nowhere.

"Now, this will be an easy village for the rebels to capture," Jumah said, laughing.

We walked around trying to find a sign of someone's presence. Some sort of production of palm oil had taken place here; there were the remains of palm nut seeds everywhere. On the river floated a deserted canoe in which spirogyra had grown. Back at the old house, we debated where to sleep. We sat outside on logs at the foot of the verandah and Musa offered to tell a story about Bra Spider.

"No!" we protested—we all knew it too well—but he still continued.

"Bra Spider stories are always good no matter how many times you have heard them," Musa said.

"My mother told me that whenever a story is told, it is worth listening to. So please listen. I will tell it quickly." He coughed and began.

"Bra Spider lived in a village that was surrounded by many other villages. At the end of the harvest season, all the villages had a feast in celebration of their successful harvest. Wine and food were in abundance and people ate until they could see their reflections on each other's stomach."

"What?" we all said in shock at this extra detail he had added to the story.

"I am telling the story, so I can tell *my* version. Wait for your turn." Musa stood up. We listened attentively to see if he was going to embellish the story with more striking details. He sat down and continued:

"Each village specialized in one dish. Bra Spider's village made okra soup with palm oil and fish. Mmm . . . mmm . . . mmm. The other villages made cassava leaves with meat, potato leaves, and so on. Each village boasted about how good their meal was going to be. All the villages had an open invitation to their feasts. But Bra Spider took it to the extreme. He wanted to be present at all the feasts. He had to come up with a plan. He began collecting ropes around his village and weaving them several months before the feast. While people carried bushels of rice, bundles of wood, to the square and women pounded rice in mortars, removing the husk from its seeds, Bra Spider was stretching the ropes on his verandah and measuring their length. When men went hunting, he was busy laying out his ropes by the paths from his village to all the surrounding villages. He gave the ends of his ropes to the chiefs, who tied them to the nearest trees at their village squares. 'Tell your people to pull the rope when their meal is ready,' he told every chief in his nasal voice. Bra Spider starved for a week as he readied himself. When the day finally came, Bra Spider rose up earlier than everyone else. He sat on his verandah and securely tied all the ropes at his waist. He was shaking and saliva dripped out of his mouth as the smell of smoked meat, dried fish, and various stews wafted out from the cooking huts.

"Unluckily for Bra Spider, all the feasts started at the same time and the chiefs ordered the ropes to be pulled. He was suspended in the air above his village, pulled from all directions. Bra Spider screamed for help, but the drums and songs from his village square drowned his voice. He could see people gathering around plates of food and licking their hands at the end of the meal. Children walked across the village on their way to the river, munching on pieces of stewed chicken, goat, and deer meat. Each time Bra Spider tried to loosen the ropes, the villages pulled harder, as they thought it was a signal that he was ready to visit their feast. At the end of the celebration in Bra Spider's village, a boy saw him and called on the elders. They cut the ropes and brought Bra Spider down. In a barely audible voice he demanded some food, but there was nothing left. The feasts had ended everywhere. Bra Spider remained hungry, and because he was pulled so tight for so long, this explains why spiders have a thin waistline."

"All this food in the story is making me hungry. Good story, though. I have never heard it told like this," Alhaji said, stretching his back. We all laughed, as we knew he was mocking Musa for adding some details to the tale.

As soon as Musa was done, night took over the village. It was as if the sky had quickly rolled over, changing its bright side to dark, bringing sleep with it for my companions. We placed the smoked meat and the gallon of water by the door of the room we occupied. I stayed in the room with my friends, even though I didn't fall asleep until the very last hours of the night. I remembered nights I had spent sitting with my grandmother by the fire. "You are growing up so fast. It feels like yesterday when I was at your name-giving ceremony." She would look at me, her shiny face glowing, before she told me the story of my name-giving ceremony. Growing up, I had been to several of these ceremonies, but Grandmother always told me about mine.

Everyone in the community was present. Before things started, food was prepared in abundance with everyone's help. Early in the morning, the men slaughtered a sheep, skinned it, and shared the meat among the finest women cooks, so that each would cook her best dish for the ceremony. While the women cooked, the men stood around in the yard welcoming each other with firm handshakes, laughing, each man clearing his throat as loud as he could before he started talking. Boys who hung about and eavesdropped on the men's conversations would be called upon to perform certain tasks—slaughter chickens behind the cooking huts, chop firewood.

Near the thatched-roof cooking huts, women sang while they pounded rice in mortars. They did tricks with pestles. They flipped them in the air and clapped several times before they caught them, and continued pounding and singing. The women who were older and more experienced not only clapped several times before they caught their pestles but also made elaborate "thank you" gestures, all in harmony with the songs they sang. Inside the huts, girls sat on the ground fanning red charcoals with a bamboo fan or an old plate, or simply by blowing to start the fire under the big pots.

By nine o'clock in the morning the food was ready. Everyone dressed up in his or her finest clothing. The women were especially elegant in their beautiful patterned cotton skirts, dresses, shirts, and *lappei*—a big cotton cloth that women wrap around their waist—and extravagant head wraps. Everyone was in high spirits and ready to commence the ceremony that was to last until noon.

"The imam arrived late," said my grandmother. A large metal tray containing *leweh* (rice paste), kola nuts lined on the side, and water in a calabash was handed over to him, and after settling himself on a stool in the middle of the yard, and rolling up the sleeves of his white gown, he mixed the *leweh* and separated it into several carefully molded portions, each topped with a kola nut. The imam then proceeded to read several suras from the Quran. After the prayer he sprinkled some water on the ground to invite the spirits of the ancestors.

The imam waved to my mother, motioning her to bring me to him. It was my first time outside in the open. My mother knelt before the imam and presented me to him. He rubbed some of the water from the calabash on my forehead and recited more prayers, followed by the proclamation of my name. "Ishmael he shall be called," he said, and everyone clapped. Women started singing and dancing. My mother passed me to my father, who raised me high above the crowd before passing me around to be held by everyone present. I had become a member of the community and was now owned and cared for by all.

The food was brought out on humongous plates. The elders started to feast first, all eating from one plate. The men did the same, then the boys, before the women and girls had their share. Singing and dancing followed the feast. While the jubilation was going on, I was placed in the hands and care of older women who couldn't dance much anymore. They held me, smiled at me, and called me "little husband." They started telling me stories about the community. Whenever I gave them a smile, they remarked, "He loves stories. Well, you came to the right place."

I smiled a bit, as I could visualize my grandmother's happy face at the end of this story. Some of my traveling companions were snoring as the late-night breeze caused my eyes to become heavy.

When we woke up the next morning, all the smoked meat was gone. We started blaming each other. Kanei inspected Musa's lips. Musa became angry, and they started throwing blows at each other. I was about to part them when Saidu pointed to the tattered bag at the edge of the verandah.

"This is the bag, right?" he said, pointing to its chewed edges. "This was not done by any of us. See, the bag is still tied." He showed it to us. "Something else ate the meat, and whatever ate this meat is still around somewhere." He picked up a stick and began walking toward the bushes.

"You see, it wasn't me." Musa pushed Kanei out of his way as he joined Saidu.

"It is some kind of animal," Moriba said, inspecting the prints the creature's feet had left on the ground. Some of us looked around the village while others followed the tracks of the creature down the path to the river. We were about to give up looking when Saidu shouted from behind the storage house in the village:

"I found the thief and he is angry."

We ran to see what it was. It was a dog munching on the last bit of the smoked meat. Upon seeing us, it began barking and guarding the meat with its hind legs.

"You bad dog. That is ours." Alhaji took the stick from Saidu and started chasing the animal. The dog still held on to the last bit of meat as it disappeared among the bushes. With a shake of the head, Saidu picked up the gallon of water and started heading down the path. We all followed him, Alhaji still holding the stick.

That afternoon we began rummaging the bushes for whatever fruit looked edible. We didn't converse much as we walked.

In the evening we stopped to rest along the path.

"I should have killed that dog," Alhaji said slowly, as he rolled on his back.

"Why?" I asked.

"Yes. Why? What good would it have done?" Moriba sat up.

"I just wanted to kill it because it ate the only food we had," Alhaji angrily replied.

"It would have made good meat," Musa said.

"I don't think so. Plus, it would have been difficult to prepare it, anyway." I turned to Musa, who was lying on his back next to me.

"You guys disgust me just thinking about something like that." Jumah spat.

"Well." Musa stood up.

"He is going to tell another story." Alhaji sighed.

Musa turned to Alhaji. "Yes, well, not really a story." He paused and then continued. "My father used to work for these Malaysians, and he told me that they ate dogs. So if Alhaji had killed that dog, I would have loved to try some. So when I see my father again, I can tell him how it tasted. And he will not be angry with me, because I had a good excuse for eating dog meat," Musa concluded.

We all became quiet, thinking about our own families. Musa had triggered in all of us what we were afraid of thinking.

Musa was home with his father in Mattru Jong when the attack took place. His mother had gone to the market to buy fish for the evening meal. He and his father had run toward the market and found his mother, but as they ran out of town, his mother had somehow been left behind. They realized that she wasn't with them only after they stopped for a rest at the first village they reached. His father cried and told Musa to stay there while he went to look for his wife. Musa told his father that he wanted to go back down the path with him. "No, my son, stay here and I'll bring back your mother." As soon as his father left, the village was attacked and Musa ran away. He had been running ever since.

Alhaji was at the river fetching water when the rebels attacked. He ran home, only to stand in front of the empty house shouting the names of his parents, two brothers, and sister.

Kanei had escaped with his parents, but lost his two sisters and three brothers in the chaos. He and his parents had jumped in a boat along with many others to cross the Jong River. When the boat reached the middle of the river, the rebels on shore began shooting at the people in the boat, and everyone panicked, causing the boat to capsize. Kanei swam to the other side of the river as fast as he could. When he pulled himself ashore, he could see people drowning in the water, screaming as they fought to stay afloat. The rebels laughed at the dying people. He had wept all night as he followed the survivors, who made their way to a village down the river. There, people had told Kanei that his parents had passed through. The hope of finding his family had kept Kanei moving over the months.

Jumah and Moriba lived next to each other. RPGs had destroyed their houses during the attack. They had run toward the wharf to find their parents, who were traders, but their parents were nowhere to be found. They ran to the forest where their families had earlier hidden, but they weren't there either.

Saidu's family was unable to leave town during the attack. Along with his parents and three sisters, who were nineteen, seventeen, and fifteen, he hid under the bed during the night. In the morning the rebels broke into the house and found his parents and three sisters. Saidu had climbed to the attic to bring down the remaining rice for their journey, when the rebels stormed in. Saidu sat in the attic, holding his breath and listening to the wailing of his sisters as the rebels raped them. His father shouted at them to stop, and one of the rebels hit him with the butt of his gun. Saidu's mother cried and apologized to her daughters for having brought them into this world to be victims of such madness. After the rebels had raped the sisters over and over, they bundled the family's property and made the father and mother carry it. They took the three girls with them.

"To this day, I carry the pain that my sisters and parents felt. When I climbed down after the rebels were gone, I couldn't stand and my tears froze in my eyes. I felt like my veins were being harshly pulled out of my body. I still feel like that all the time, as I can't stop thinking about that day. What did my sisters do to anyone?" Saidu said after he was done telling us the story one night in an abandoned village. My teeth became sour as I listened to his story. It was then that I understood why he was so quiet all the time.

"We should keep walking," Kanei said sadly as he dusted his pants. We had agreed to walk at night. During the day we would search for food and take turns sleeping. At night it felt as if we were walking with the moon. It followed us under thick clouds and waited for us at the other end of dark forest paths. It would disappear with sunrise but return again, hovering on our path, the next night. Its brightness became dull as nights passed. Some nights the sky wept stars that quickly floated and disappeared into the darkness before our wishes could meet them. Under these stars and sky I used to hear stories, but now it seemed as if it was the sky that was telling us a story as its stars fell, violently colliding with each other. The moon hid behind clouds to avoid seeing what was happening.

During the day the sun refused to rise gradually, as it had before. It became bright from the minute it surfaced from behind the clouds, its golden rays darkening my eyes. The clouds in the blue sky sailed violently, destroying each other's formation.

One afternoon, while we were searching for food in a deserted village, a crow fell out of the sky. It wasn't dead, but it was unable to fly. We knew this was unusual, but we needed food and anything at that point would do. As we took the feathers off the bird, Moriba asked what day it was. We all thought about it for a while, trying to remember the name of the last day when our lives were normal. Kanei broke the silence.

"It is a holiday." He laughed. "You can call it any day you want," he continued.

"But it is not just a day, it is a strange one. I don't feel too good about it," Musa said. "Maybe we shouldn't eat this bird."

"Well now, if the falling of this bird is a sign of a curse or bad luck, we are in both. So I am eating every bit of it. You can do as you please." Kanei began humming.

After Kanei stopped humming, the world became eerily silent. The breeze and the clouds had stopped moving, the trees were still, as if they all awaited something unimaginable.

Sometimes night has a way of speaking to us, but we almost never listen. The night after we ate the bird was too dark. There were no stars in the sky, and as we walked, it seemed as if the darkness was getting thicker. We weren't on a dense forest path, but we could barely see each other. We held on to one another's hands. We kept on walking because we couldn't stop in the middle of nowhere, even though we wanted to. After hours of walking we came upon a bridge made of sticks. The river below was flowing quietly, as if asleep. As we were about to set foot on the bridge, we heard footsteps on the other side, coming toward us. We let go of one another's hands and hid in the nearby bushes. I was lying with Alhaji, Jumah, and Saidu.

There were three people. They were wearing white shirts. Two of them were about the same height and the third was shorter. They carried cloths under their arms. They too were holding hands, and when they stepped off the bridge around where we lay, they stopped as if they sensed our presence. They mumbled something. It was difficult to hear what they were saying because their voices sounded like bees, as if something was obstructing their noses. After they were done mumbling, the two taller people began pulling the shorter one. One wanted them to go the way we were going and the other insisted that they continue in the opposite direction. Their quarrel caused my heart to begin beating faster, and I was trying hard to make out their faces, but it was too dark. After about a minute, they decided to continue going in the direction we had come from.

It took us a few minutes to rise from under the bushes. Everyone was breathing hard and couldn't speak. Kanei began whispering our names. When he called out Saidu's name, Saidu didn't answer. We searched for him among the bushes. He was lying there quietly. We shook him hard, calling out his name, but he was silent. Alhaji and Jumah began to cry. Kanei and I dragged Saidu onto the path and sat by him. He was just lying there. My hands began trembling uncontrollably as we sat there throughout the night in silence. My head became heavy as I thought about what we were going to do. I do not remember who it was among us that whispered, "Maybe it was the bird that we ate." Most of my travel companions began to cry, but I couldn't. I just sat there staring into the night as if searching for something.

There wasn't a gradual change between night and day. The darkness just swiftly rolled away, letting the sky shine its light on us. We were all sitting in the middle of the path. Saidu was still quiet. His forehead had residues of sweat and his mouth was slightly open. I put my hand by his nose just to see if he was breathing. Everyone stood up, and when I removed my hand, they were all looking at me, as if expecting me to say something.

"I don't know," I said.

They all put their hands on their heads. Their faces looked as if they wanted to hear something else, something that we knew could be possible but were afraid to accept.

"What are we going to do now?" Moriba asked.

"We cannot just stand here forever," Musa remarked.

"We will have to carry him to the next village, however far that might be," Kanei said slowly. "Help me stand him up," he continued.

We stood Saidu up, and Kanei carried him on his back across the bridge. The quiet river started flowing loudly through rocks and palm kernels. As soon as we had crossed the bridge, Saidu coughed. Kanei set him down and we all gathered around him. He vomited for a few minutes, and wiping his mouth, he said, "Those were ghosts last night. I know it."

We all agreed with him.

"I must have fainted after they started speaking." He tried to get up, and we all aided him.

"I am fine. Let's go." He pushed us away.

"You woke from the dead with some attitude," Musa said.

We all laughed and started walking. My hands began trembling again, I didn't know why this time. It was a gloomy day and we kept asking Saidu if he was okay all the way to the next village.

It was past midday when we arrived at a crowded village. We were shocked by how noisy it was in the middle of the war. It was the biggest village we had been to so far. It sounded like a marketplace. People were playing music and dancing, children were running around, and there was that familiar good smell of cooked cassava leaf in rich palm oil.

As we walked through the village trying to find a place to sit away from the crowd, we saw some familiar faces. People hesitantly waved to us. We found a log under a mango tree and sat down. A woman whose face wasn't among the familiar ones came and sat facing us.

"You." She pointed at me. "I know you," she said.

I did not know her face, but she insisted that she knew my family and me. She told me that Junior had come to the village a few weeks earlier looking for me and that she had also seen my mother, father, and little brother in the next village, which was about two days' walk. She told us the direction and ended by saying, "In that village there are lots of people from Mattru Jong and the Sierra Rutile mining area. All of you might be able to find your families or news about them."

She got up and began dancing to the *soukous* music that was playing as she left us. We all began laughing. I wanted to leave right away, but we decided to spend the night in the village. Also, we wanted Saidu to rest, even though he kept telling us that he was fine. I was so happy that my mother, father, and two brothers had somehow found one another. Perhaps my mother and father have gotten back together, I thought.

We went to the river for a swim, and there we played hide-and-seek swimming games, running along the river's edge screaming "*Cocoo*" to commence the game. Everyone was smiling.

That night we stole a pot of rice and cassava leaves. We ate it under coffee trees at the edge of the village, washed the pots, and returned them. We had no place to sleep, so we chose a verandah on one of the houses after everyone had gone inside.

I didn't sleep that night. My hands began shaking as soon as my friends started snoring. I had a feeling that something bad was going to happen. The dogs began to cry and ran from one end of the village to the other.

Alhaji woke up and sat by me. "The dogs woke me up," he said.

"I couldn't sleep to begin with," I replied.

"Maybe you are just anxious about seeing your family." He chuckled. "I am, too."

Alhaji stood up. "Don't you think it is strange, the way the dogs are crying?"

One dog had come near the verandah on which we sat and was vigorously crying. A few more dogs joined in. Their crying pierced my heart.

"Yes. They sound very human," I said.

"That is the same thing I was thinking." Alhaji yawned. "I think dogs see things we do not see. Something must be wrong." He sat down.

We became quiet, just staring into the night. The dogs cried all night long, one continuing till the sky was completely clear. Babies then began to take up the cry. People started getting up, so we had to vacate the verandah. Alhaji and I began waking our friends. When he shook Saidu, Saidu was still.

"Get up, we have to go now." He shook Saidu harder as we heard the people on whose verandah we had slept getting ready to come outside.

"Saidu, Saidu," Kanei coaxed him. "Maybe he fainted again," he said.

A man came out and greeted us. He carried a small bucket of water. He had a smile on his face that told us he had known all along that we were on the verandah.

"This will do it." The man sprinkled some of the cold water from his bucket on Saidu.

But Saidu didn't move. He just lay on his stomach, his face buried in the dust. His palms were turned upside down and they were pale. The man turned him around and checked his pulse. Saidu's forehead was sweaty and wrinkled. His mouth was slightly opened and there was a path of dried tears at the corners of his eyes down to his cheeks.

"Do you boys know anyone in this village?" the man asked.

We all said no, shaking our heads. He exhaled heavily, put his bucket down, and placed both his hands on his head.

"Who is the oldest?" he asked, looking at Alhaji.

Kanei raised his hand. They stepped outside the verandah and the man whispered something in his ear. Kanei began to cry on the man's shoulder. It was then that we admitted that Saidu had left us. Everyone else was crying, but I couldn't cry. I felt dizzy and my eyes watered. My hands began shaking again. I felt the warmth inside my stomach, and my heart was beating slowly, but at a heavy rate. The man and Kanei walked away, and when they returned, they brought with them two men, who carried a wooden stretcher. They placed Saidu on it and asked us to follow them.

Saidu's body was washed and prepared for burial that same day. He was wrapped in white linen and placed in a wooden coffin that was set on a table in the living room of the man whose verandah we had slept on.

"Are any of you his family?" a tall, slender, muscular man asked. He was in charge of the burial ceremonies in the village. We all shook our heads no. I felt as if we were denying Saidu, our friend, our traveling companion. He had become our family, but the man wanted a real family member who could authorize his burial.

"Does any one of you know his family?" The man looked at us.

"I do." Kanei raised his hand.

The man called him over to where he stood on the other side of the coffin. They began talking. I tried to figure out what they were saying by reading the elaborate gestures that the man made with his right hand. His left hand was on Kanei's shoulder. Kanei's lips moved for a while, and then he began nodding until the conversation was over.

Kanei came back and sat with us on the stools that were provided for the funeral service, which only we attended, along with the man on whose verandah Saidu had left us. The rest of the people in the village quietly sat on their verandahs. They stood up as we walked through part of the village to the cemetery.

I was in disbelief that Saidu had actually left us. I held on to the idea that he had just fainted and would get up soon. It hit me that he wasn't going to get up only after he was lowered into the hole, just in the shroud, and the diggers started covering him with the earth. What was left of him was only a memory. The glands in my throat began to hurt. I couldn't breathe well, so I opened my mouth. The man who had asked earlier if any of us were Saidu's family began to read suras. It was then that I began to weep quietly. I let my tears drip on the earth and the summer dust absorb them. The men who had carried Saidu began placing rocks around the grave to hold the mounds of earth.

After the burial, we were the only ones left in the cemetery. There were mounds of earth all over. Very few had sticks with something written on them. The rest were anonymous. Saidu had just joined them. We sat in the cemetery for hours, as if expecting something. But we were young—all of us were now thirteen, except for Kanei, who was three years older—and our emotions were in disarray. I couldn't comprehend what or how I felt. This confusion hurt my head and made my stomach tense. We left the cemetery as night approached. It was quiet in the village. We sat outside on the log we had first sat on when we entered the village. None of us thought of going to sleep on a verandah. Kanei explained to us that Saidu had had to be buried, as the custom in the village was that the dead couldn't be kept overnight. It was either that or we would have had to take Saidu out of the village. No one responded to Kanei. He stopped talking and the dogs began to cry again. They did all night, until we became restless.

We walked up and down the village. Most people weren't asleep; we could hear them whispering when the dogs took breaks or went to cry on opposite ends of the village. I remembered a few weeks back when Saidu had spoken about parts of him slowly dying each passing day, as we carried on with our journey. Perhaps all of him had died that night when he spoke in that strange voice after we had survived that attack by men with machetes, axes, and spears, I thought. My hands and feet began to shake, and they continued to do so throughout the night. I was worried and kept calling out my friends' names, so that they wouldn't fall asleep. I was afraid if any did, he was going to leave us. Early in the morning, Kanei told us that we were going to leave after sunrise and head for the next village. "I can't stand another night listening to these dogs. They terrify me," he said.

That morning we thanked the men who had helped bury Saidu. "You will always know where he is laid," one of the men said. I nodded in agreement, but I knew that the chances of coming back to the village were slim, as we had no control over our future. We knew only how to survive.

As we left the village, everyone lined up to watch us go. I was scared, as this reminded me of when we had walked through the village with Saidu's body. We went by the cemetery, which was at the edge of town, by the path that led to where we hoped to reunite with our families. The sun penetrated the graveyard, and as we stood there, a slight breeze blew, causing the trees surrounding the mounds of earth to sway gracefully. I felt a chill at the back of my neck, as if someone were softly blowing on me. A strand of smoke was rising from the village, making its way to the sky. I watched it as it disappeared. We were leaving our friend, or as my grandmother would put it, "His temporary journey in this world had ended." We, on the other hand, had to continue.

When we started to walk away, we all began to sob. The cockcrows faded, only to make us aware of our silence, the silence that asked, Who will be next to leave us? The question was in our eyes when we looked at each other. We walked fast as if trying to stay in the daytime, afraid that nightfall would turn over the uncertain pages of our lives.

11

━━━◆━━━

WE HAD BEEN WALKING in silence through the night until we stopped to listen to the singing of morning birds shattering the silence of the day. As we sat on the side of the path, Moriba began to sob. He was sitting away from us, something he usually did with Saidu. He played with a piece of branch, trying to distract himself from what he was feeling. Everyone except me started to sob and moved next to Moriba, who was now crying loudly. I sat by myself, covering my face with the palms of my hands to hold back my tears. After a few minutes, my friends stopped crying. We continued on without saying a word to each other. We all knew that we could grieve only for a short while in order to continue staying alive.

"I look forward to getting to this village. Ah, I will give my mother a very tight hug." Alhaji smiled and then continued. "She always complains, though, when I give her a tight hug: 'If you love me, stop squeezing my old bones so I can be alive longer.' She is funny."

We giggled.

"I have a feeling that we will find our families, or at least news of them." Kanei stretched his hands as if trying to catch the sun. He looked at Alhaji, who was smiling uncontrollably. "I heard you have a beautiful sister. I am still just your friend, right?" We all started laughing. Alhaji jumped on Kanei's back, and they began to wrestle in the grass. When they were done, they followed us on the path, singing one of S. E. Rogie's songs, "*Nor look me bad eye, nor weigh me lek dat . . .*" We joined in and sang as if we were having one of life's most glorious moments. But slowly silence returned and took over.

One side of the sky was completely blue and the other was filled with stagnant clouds. The quiet breeze caused a branch to snap in the forest. The echo sounded like a cry, a wailing. I wasn't the only one who noticed it, because my friends stopped briefly and listened attentively. The breeze picked up its pace. The leaves of the trees began to rub against each other, resisting the wind. More branches snapped in the forest and the wailing intensified. The trees looked as if they were in pain. They swayed in all directions and slapped each other with their branches. The clouds rolled over the blue sky and it became dark. A heavy rain followed, with thunder and lightning that lasted for less than fifteen minutes. Afterward, the sky returned to its bluest. I walked, perplexed, in my soaked clothes under the sun. At nighttime it began to rain again. The strands of rain fell brutally from the sky, whipping us. We walked for most of the night, wiping the water off our faces in order to see. It became unbearable to continue, so we sat at the foot of huge trees and waited. Whenever the lightning lit the forest, I could see where everyone was sitting. We all had our faces resting on our knees and our arms were crossed.

The last hours of the night were long. By the time the rain stopped, it was light. We were all shivering, our fingertips pale and wrinkled.

"We look like soaked chickens," Musa said, laughing, as we emerged from under the trees. We found an opening where the sun had begun penetrating, and we squeezed and spread our shirts on the tops of the bushes and sat in the sun to dry ourselves.

It was almost midday when we put on our damp clothes and continued walking. A few hours later we heard a cockcrow in the distance. Musa jumped in the air and we all began to laugh.

Finally, we were approaching the village where seeing our families was actually a possibility. I couldn't stop smiling. Coffee trees began to replace forest, and footprints appeared on the path. We heard rice being pounded and whispers in the breeze. We quickened our pace as these sounds assured us that life was ahead. On the opposite side of the coffee farm was a small banana farm, and there we came across a man cutting down hands of ripe bananas. We couldn't see his face, as his head was behind the leaves.

"Good afternoon," Kanei said.

The man peeped at us from behind a banana leaf. He wiped the sweat off his forehead and walked toward us. As he approached, slowly making his way through the noisy dried banana leaves, the sight of his face awakened my memory.

His face was a little wrinkled now and he was much skinnier than when I had last seen him. His name was Gasemu, Ngor* Gasemu. He used to be one of the notorious single men in my town. Back then, everyone talked about him not being married. The older people always remarked, "He is old enough and responsible enough to find himself a good wife, but he likes to be alone, he likes that loose life." He never said anything back then and didn't get upset by what they said. He cooked his own food, and when he was too tired to cook, he ate *gari*† with honey. There was a period of time when he ate *gari* with honey for over a week. My mother decided to dish him out a plate every evening. "That food is unhealthy for you," she had said to him, and he smiled, rubbing his head.

When Gasemu was by the path, he stopped and examined our faces. He smiled, and that was when I became sure that he was the Ngor Gasemu I knew, because he was missing a front tooth.

"You boys want to help me carry some bananas to the village?" he

*A respectful term placed before the first name of adults.

†A grated and dried food made from cassava.

asked in that manner that adults usually ask young people, so that we knew he wouldn't take no for an answer.

"Come on, boys." He motioned for us to follow him into the banana farm. All of us started walking past him as he continued waving his hand as if he was pulling us with an invisible rope. When I approached him, he put his hand on my shoulder and rubbed my head.

"Are you still a troublesome boy?" He pulled on my nose.

"There is no time to be troublesome these days," I said.

"I see that you look very sad. Your forehead used to glow naturally when you were just a child. Your parents and I used to discuss how unusual that was. We thought it was because you were happy all the time. Your mother said you even smiled while you slept. But when you started your troublesomeness and were angry, your forehead glowed even more. We didn't have any other explanations for your forehead and how it related to your character. And here you are, it isn't shining anymore." He paused for a moment, looking at me.

He walked away and began instructing my traveling companions how to pick up a hand of bananas and carry it on their shoulders instead of their heads. "This way you won't break them in half," he explained.

I picked up some of the bananas and waited for Gasemu to gather his water jug, machete, and the last bunch. "So how did you get . . ." I started, but he interrupted.

"Your parents and brothers will be happy to see you. They have been talking about you every day and praying for your safety. Your mother cries every day, begging the gods and ancestors to return you to her. Your older brother left to look for you, but he returned about a week ago. His face was sad when he returned. I think he blames himself for losing you."

I dropped the hand as he started giving me this news. He continued walking, so I quickly picked up the bananas and followed him. "They will indeed be surprised to see you."

He walked slowly in front of me. I was breathing fast and couldn't bring out a word. I wanted to drop the hand and run as fast as I could to the village. My eyelids were twitching, and I felt as if the breeze was passing through my brain. It made me feel light-headed. Excitement and sadness made me feel as if my heart would explode if I waited any longer, but on such a narrow path I couldn't walk past all those in front of me.

After a few minutes we came to a river and I was happy, because at the edge of most villages there was a river, so I thought we should be there any minute now. But we weren't yet.

"The village is just over the hill," Gasemu said. It was a long hill, with rocks on either side of the path and some unmovable ones the road makers had left in the middle. The path zigzagged up to the top, where, when we finally made it, everyone had to rest for a few minutes. I became angry that we had to rest, and I sat on a big rock away from the group. My eyes followed the brown dusty path that continued down the hill to the thick forest, through which I caught a glimpse of the thatched and tin roofs of the village. Part of me was on the way to the village, the other impatiently waited on the hill. Gasemu passed around his jug of water, which I refused. When it got back to him, we picked up the banana hands and started down the hill. I started before everyone else, so that I could walk fast and be in front.

As I was going down the hill, I heard gunshots. And dogs barking. And people screaming and crying. We dropped the bananas and began running in order to avoid the open hillside. A thick smoke started rising from the village. At the top of it, sparks of flames leapt into the air.

We hid in the nearby bushes and listened to gunshots and the screams of men, women, and children. The children wailed, men screamed at high pitches that pierced through the forest and covered the shrieks of women. The gunshots finally ceased, and the world was very quiet, as if listening. I told Gasemu that I wanted to go to the village. He held me back, but I shoved him into the bushes and ran down the path as fast as I could. I didn't feel my legs. When I got to the village, it was completely on fire and bullet shells covered the ground like mango leaves in the morning. I did not know where to begin looking for my family. Gasemu and my friends had followed me, and we all stood looking at the flaming village. I was sweating because of the heat, but I wasn't afraid to run in between the houses. Nails were popping off tin roofs, and they flew, landing on nearby thatched roofs, increasing the wrath of the fire. As we were watching a flaming tin roof in flight, we heard screams and loud banging a few houses away. We ran behind the houses at the edge of the coffee trees and came upon the house where the cries were coming from. There were people locked in it. The fire was already too much inside. It showed its face through the windows and the roof. We picked up a mortar and banged the door open, but it was too late. Only two people came out, a woman and a young child. They were on fire, and ran up and down the village, slamming themselves against everything in their way and going back in the other direction to do the same. The woman fell and stopped moving. The child gave a loud screech and sat next to a tree. He stopped moving. It all happened so fast that we just stood there, rooted to the ground. The child's yelp was still echoing in my head, as if it had taken on a life of its own inside me.

Gasemu had wandered away from where I stood. He began screaming from another side of the village. We ran to where he was. More than twenty people lay facedown in the earth. They were all lined up, and blood still poured out of their bullet wounds. A stream of it had begun running along the ground, making its way under each body, as if joining them together. Gasemu's sobs grew louder as he turned each body over. Some of their mouths and eyes were open in shapes that showed how much they had cringed as they waited for the bullets from behind. Some had inhaled dirt, perhaps while taking their last breath. The bodies were mostly men in their late and early twenties. A few were younger.

On other paths of the village were the half-burnt remains of those who had fought fiercely to free themselves, only to die outside. They lay on the ground in different postures of pain, some reaching for their heads, the white bones in their jaws visible, others curled up like a child in a womb, frozen.

The fire had begun to die down, and I was running around the village looking for something, something I did not want to see. I hesitantly tried to make out the faces of burnt bodies, but it was impossible to tell who they had been. Besides, there were too many of them.

"They stayed in that house," Gasemu said to me as he pointed toward one of the charred houses. The fire had consumed all the door and window frames, and the mud that had been pushed in between the sticks was falling off, revealing the ropes through which the remaining fire was making its way.

My entire body went into shock. Only my eyes moved, slowly opening and closing. I tried to shake my legs to get my blood flowing, but I fell to the ground, holding my face. On the ground I felt as if my eyes were growing too big for their sockets. I could feel them expanding, and the pain released my body from the shock. I ran toward the house. Without any fear I went inside and looked around the smoke-filled rooms. The floors were filled with heaps of ashes; no solid form of a body was inside. I screamed at the top of my lungs and began to cry as loudly as I could, punching and kicking with all my might into the weak walls that continued to burn. I had lost my sense of touch. My hands and feet punched and kicked the burning walls, but I couldn't feel a thing. Gasemu and the rest of the other boys began pulling me away from the house. I kept kicking and punching as they dragged me out.

"I have looked around for them, but I can't see them anywhere," Gasemu said. I was sitting on the ground with my legs spread in the dirt, holding my head in my hands. I was filled up with anger. I hissed and boiled, and my heart felt as if it was going to explode. At the same time, I felt as if something had literally been placed on my head, heavier than I could ever imagine, and my neck was beginning to ache.

If we hadn't stopped to rest on that hill, if we hadn't run into Gasemu, I would have seen my family, I thought. My head was burning as if on fire. I put my hands on both ears and squeezed them in vain. I didn't know what was happening to me. I got up, walked behind Gasemu, and locked his neck under my arms. I squeezed him as hard as I could. "I can't breathe," he said, fighting back. He pushed me off, and I fell next to a pestle. I picked it up and hit Gasemu with it. He fell, and when he got up, his nose was bleeding. My friends held me back. Gasemu looked at me and said sadly, "I didn't know this was going to happen." He walked toward a mango tree and sat by it, wiping the blood falling from his nose.

My friends had pinned me to the ground and were vehemently arguing. Some said it was Gasemu's fault that we didn't get to see our parents. Others said it wasn't, and that if it hadn't been for him, we would all be dead. I didn't care. I wanted to see my family, even if it meant dying with them. My friends started fighting among themselves, kicking, punching, throwing each other to the ground. Alhaji pushed Jumah into one of the houses and his pants caught on fire. He screamed as he rolled in the dirt, slapping the fire off. When Jumah got up, he picked up a stone and threw it at Alhaji. It hit Alhaji on the back of his head. Blood ran down his neck. When Alhaji saw his blood, he became furious and ran toward Jumah, but Gasemu intervened. He pulled Alhaji away and tied his bleeding head with a piece of cloth. We were all quiet and angry in the ruins of the village, where it seemed our journey had ended.

"None of this is anyone's fault," Gasemu said slowly. His words made me angry, and I wanted to rush him again. But we heard loud voices of people approaching the village. We ran into the nearby coffee farm and lay in the dirt watching the village.

A group of more than ten rebels walked into the village. They were laughing and giving each other high fives. Two looked slightly older than me. They had blood on their clothes, and one of them carried the head of a man, which he held by the hair. The head looked as if it was still feeling its hair being pulled. Blood dripped from where the neck had once been. The other rebel carried a gallon of gasoline and a big box of matches. The rebels sat on the ground and started playing cards, smoking marijuana, and boasting about what they had done that day.

"We burned about three villages today." One skinny guy, who was perhaps enjoying himself more than everyone else, laughed.

Another rebel, the only one dressed in full army gear, agreed with him. "Yes, three is impressive, in just a few hours in the afternoon." He paused, playing with the side of his G3 weapon. "I especially enjoyed burning this village. We caught everyone here. No one escaped. That is how good it was. We carried out the command and executed everyone. Commander will be pleased when he gets here." He nodded, looking at the rest of the rebels, who had stopped the game to listen to him. They all agreed with him, nodding their heads. They gave each other high fives and resumed their game.

"Some people escaped in the other two villages," the other rebel who was standing up said. He paused, rubbing his forehead, as if pondering why that had happened, and then continued: "They probably saw the smoke from this village and knew something was happening. We should change our strategy. Next time we must attack all the villages at the same time." The others didn't pay him as much attention as they did when the rebel dressed in the army suit spoke. The rebels went on with their card games, chatting for hours, and then for no apparent reason they shot a couple of rounds into the air. Someone in my group moved and the dried coffee leaves made some noise. The rebels stopped playing their game and ran in different directions to take cover. Two started walking toward us, aiming their guns. They walked fast and then crouched. As if planned, we all got up and started running. Bullets followed us out of the coffee farm and into the forest. Gasemu was in front and he knew where he was going. We all followed him.

When we reached the forest's edge, Gasemu stopped and waited for us to catch up. "Follow the path straight," he told us. When I reached him he tried to smile at me. I do not know why, but it made me angrier. I ran past him and followed the narrow path on which grass had grown. I was behind Alhaji, who parted the bushes like a diver heading to the surface for air. Some of the bushes slapped me, but I didn't stop. The gunshots grew louder behind us. We ran for hours, deeper into the forest. The path had ended, but we kept running until the sky swallowed the sun and gave birth to the moon. The bullets continued to fly behind us, but now their redness could be seen as they pierced through the bushes. The moon disappeared and took the stars with it, making the sky weep. Its tears saved us from the red bullets.

We spent the night breathing heavily under bushes soaked with rain. The hunters had given up. Gasemu began to cry like a child. It always made me afraid when such things happened. In my younger years I had learned that grown men cry only when they have no other choice. Gasemu rolled on the ground in pain. When we finally summoned the courage to pick him up, we found out why he was crying. He had been shot sometime as we ran away the previous night. His right leg was bleeding and had begun to swell. He was holding his side and didn't want to remove his hand. Alhaji lifted Gasemu's hand; his side was bleeding as well. It was as if his hand had been holding his blood from flowing. It rushed out of him like water breaking banks. He began to sweat. Alhaji asked me to contain the blood by placing my hand on Gasemu's side. I did, but his blood continued to slip through my fingers. He looked at me, his eyes sadly beginning to sink deeper into their sockets. He managed to raise his weak right hand to hold the wrist of my hand that was on his side. He had stopped sobbing, even though tears still ran down his eyes, but not as much as the blood that he was losing. Musa couldn't bear the sight of blood any longer. He fainted. Alhaji and I took Gasemu's shirt off and tied it around his side to contain his blood. The rest of our companions watched with tense faces. Musa woke up and joined them.

In between Gasemu's gasps, he told us that there was a *wahlee** nearby and that if we went back toward the farm, he would show us how to rejoin the path and get to it. We had taken the wrong turn during the night. Gasemu put his arms around my shoulder and Alhaji's. We lifted him up and began walking slowly through the bushes. We set him down every few minutes and wiped his sweaty forehead.

It was past midday when Gasemu began heaving, his entire body

---

*A place outside villages where people processed coffee or other crops.

shaking. He asked us to set him down. He held his stomach and began to roll in pain from one side to the other. His heaving increased, and he stopped rolling. He lay flat on his back, staring at the sky. His eyes were fixed on something and his legs vibrated and stopped, his hands did the same, and then finally his fingers, but his eyes remained open, transfixed on the top of the forest.

"Let's pick him up." Alhaji's voice was shaking. I put Gasemu's arm around my neck. Alhaji did the same, and we walked with him, his feet dragging on the ground. His arms were cold. His body was still sweating and he continued bleeding. We didn't say a word to each other. We all knew what had happened.

When we finally got to the *wahlee*, Gasemu's eyes were still open. Alhaji closed them. I sat by him. His blood was on my palm and my wrist. I regretted hitting him with the pestle. The dry blood was still in his nose. I began to cry softly. I couldn't cry as much as I wanted to. The sun was getting ready to leave the sky. It had come out to take Gasemu with it. I just sat by him, unable to think. My face began to harden. When the breeze blew against it, I felt how my flesh resisted enjoying the cool wind. All through the night no sleep came to me. My eyes watered and dried over and over again. I did not know what to say. For a few minutes I tried to imagine what it felt like for Gasemu when his fingers vibrated to let the last air out of his body.

12

WE MUST HAVE BEEN walking for days, I do not really remember, when suddenly two men put us at gunpoint and motioned, with their guns, for us to come closer. We walked in between two rows of men carrying machine guns, AK-47s, G3s, and RPGs. Their faces were dark, as if they had bathed them in charcoal, and they stared intensely at us with their extremely red eyes. When we got to the back of the line, there were four men lying on the ground, their uniforms soaked with blood. One of them lay on his stomach, and his eyes were wide open and still; his insides were spilling onto the ground. I turned away, and my eyes caught the smashed head of another man. Something inside his brain was still pulsating and he was breathing. I felt nauseated. Everything began to spin around me. One of the soldiers was looking at me, chewing something and smiling. He took a drink from his water bottle and threw the remaining water at my face.

"You will get used to it, everybody does eventually," he said.

Gunshots erupted nearby, and the soldiers began to move, taking the six of us with them. We came upon a river where the soldiers' aluminum boats, with motors, gently floated. We saw bodies of eleven- and thirteen-year-old boys in army shorts piled by the river. We turned our faces away. The gunshots were getting louder. As we climbed into the boats, an RPG flew from the bushes, exploding on the shore. The top of the river was boiling. A man in army trousers came running down the path toward the boats, shooting at the soldiers. One of the men in my boat opened fire, dropping the man on the ground. The boats headed downstream, and we were let off near a tributary. A soldier led us to Yele, a village that was occupied by the military. It was a big village with more than ten houses. The soldiers occupied most of them. They had cut down the bush around the village except for the entrance from the river through which we arrived. This way, the soldiers explained to us, it would be difficult for the enemy to attack.

In the beginning, it seemed we had finally found safety at Yele. The village was always full of lively chattering and laughter. The adults, civilians and soldiers, spoke about the weather, planting seasons, hunting, and nothing about the war. At first we couldn't understand why people behaved this way. But gradually the smiles on people's faces assured us that there was nothing to worry about anymore. All that darkened the mood of the village was the sight of orphaned children. There were over thirty boys between the ages of seven and sixteen. I was one of them. Apart from this, there were no indications that our childhood was threatened, much less that we would be robbed of it.

We stayed in a big unfinished cement-brick house along with other boys. A large green tarp served as its roof, and we slept on the cement floor on tiny blankets that two people shared. The soldiers set up their garrison in another unfinished brick house, and there they socialized separate from the civilians. In the evenings they watched movies, played music, laughed, and smoked marijuana. The smell of it covered the entire village. During the day they mingled with the civilians, and we helped in the kitchen. Kanei and I fetched water and washed dishes. The rest of our friends helped by chopping eggplants, onions, meat, and the like in the kitchen. I liked busying myself with work all day, going back and forth to the river and continuously washing dishes. It was the only way I could distract myself from the thoughts that were giving me severe headaches. But by midday all the daily chores were done; the evening meal was prepared and only awaited consumption. Everyone sat on the verandahs of the houses facing the village square. Parents picked their children's hair, girls played singing and clapping games, and some of the young soldiers played soccer with the boys. Their jubilation and clapping could be heard far down the river. Life was not lived in fear during the day in this village.

The soccer games reminded me of the league matches I used to play in when my family first moved to the mining town of Mogbwemo. In particular, I remembered a final match that my team, which consisted of Junior and some friends, won. Both my parents were at the game, and at the end, my mother applauded and smiled widely, her face glowing with pride. My father walked up to me and rubbed my head before he held my right hand and raised it up, as he declared me his champion. He did the same to Junior. My mother brought us a cup of water, and as we drank she fanned us with her head cloth. The excitement caused my heart to pound faster and I was sweating profusely. I could taste the salty sweat that ran from my forehead to my lips. Standing there with my family, I felt light, as if I were getting ready to fly. I wanted to hold the moment longer, not only to celebrate our victory, but because the smile on my parents' faces that evening made me so happy that I felt every nerve in my body had awoken and swayed to the gentlest wind that sailed within me.

I distanced myself from games in the village and sat behind houses, staring into the open space until my migraines temporarily subsided. I didn't tell anyone what was happening to me. My symptoms weren't mentioned in the morning when the "sergeant doctor"—as the civilians called him—lined up children and families for treatment. The sergeant doctor called for fever, cold, and many other illnesses, but he never asked if anyone was having nightmares or migraines.

At night, Alhaji, Jumah, Moriba, and Kanei played marbles on the cement floor under the moonlight that made its way through the open windowpanes. Musa had grown popular among the boys and would always end the night with a different story. I quietly sat in the corner

of the room clenching my teeth, as I didn't want to show my friends
the pain I felt from my headache. In my mind's eye I would see sparks
of flame, flashes of scenes I had witnessed, and the agonizing voices of
children and women would come alive in my head. I cried quietly as
my head beat like the clapper of a bell. Sometimes after the migraine
had stopped, I was able to fall asleep briefly, only to be awoken by
nightmares. One night I dreamt that I was shot in the head. I was lying in my blood as people hurriedly walked past me. A dog came by
and began licking my blood ferociously. The dog bared its teeth as my
blood sweetened its mouth. I wanted to scare it away, but I was unable
to move. I woke up before it started what I was afraid it was going to
do to me. I was sweating and couldn't sleep for the rest of the night.

One morning the atmosphere in the village suddenly became tense. It
wasn't clear what had caused the change, but something was about to
happen. All the soldiers assembled at the village square, dressed in their
uniforms, carrying their weapons and ammunition in backpacks and
waist belts. Their bayonets hung by the sides of their army trousers as
they stood still, with their helmets underneath their arms. "Attention."
"At ease." "Attention." "At ease." I heard the voice of the drill instructor as I walked to the river with Alhaji to fetch water. When we returned, the drill instructor had stopped warming up the soldiers.
Instead, Lieutenant Jabati stood in front of his men, his hands crossed
behind his back. He addressed them for hours before they were
released for lunch. While the lieutenant was talking to his men, we
quietly went about our daily chores and at the same time tried to
eavesdrop on what he was saying, but in order to hear him, we would
have had to get closer and join the line of soldiers, which was out of
the question. We walked about all day quietly speculating about what
the lieutenant could have told his men.

In the evening the soldiers cleaned their guns, sometimes firing a
couple of rounds into the air. These random gunshots sent the younger
children diving between the legs of their parents. The soldiers smoked
cigarettes and marijuana; some sat alone, while others gambled and

joked with one another into the night. Some watched a movie under one of their big tents.

Lieutenant Jabati sat on the verandah of his house and read a book. He would not look up, not even when his men whistled loudly at the size and sophistication of a gun in the war movie they were watching. He looked up only when it was quiet. He caught me looking at him and called me to sit with him. He was a tall man, with barely any hair. His eyes were big and they complemented his full cheekbones, which looked as if he had something in his mouth. He was a quiet individual, but his quietness had a forceful authority that all his men feared and respected. His face was so dark that it took courage to have any eye contact with him.

"Are you getting enough to eat here?" he asked.

"Yes," I said, as I tried to look at what he was reading.

"It is Shakespeare." He showed me the cover. "*Julius Caesar.* Have you heard of it?"

"I read *Julius Caesar* in school," I told him.

"Do you remember any of it?" he asked.

"Cowards die many times before their deaths . . ." I began, and he recited the whole speech with me. As soon as we were done, his face resumed its sternness. He ignored me and seemed to delve into his book. I watched as the veins on his forehead became transparent through his flesh and disappeared as he absorbed the contents of the book or thought about whatever else was on his mind. I tiptoed away from him as the sky exchanged sunlight for darkness.

When I was seven, I used to go to the town square to recite monologues from the works of Shakespeare for the adults of my community. At the end of every week, the male adults would gather to discuss matters of the community. They sat on long wooden benches, and at the end of their discussions I would be called upon to recite Shakespeare. My father would cough loudly to alert the other adults to be silent so that I could start. He sat in the front, with his arms crossed and a big smile on his face that looked as if it would take years to fade away. I stood on a bench and held on to a long stick as my sword. I would then start with *Julius Caesar*. "Friends, Romans, countrymen, lend me your ears . . ." I always recited speeches from *Macbeth* and *Julius Caesar*, as those were the adults' favorites. I was always eager and excited to read for them, because it made me feel that I was really good at speaking the English language.

I was awake when the soldiers left in the middle of the night, the echo of their marching leaving an eerie air about the village that continued until dawn and through the rest of the day. There were ten soldiers left behind to protect the village, and they stood at their posts all day. Just when the evening was waving its fingers, signaling night to approach, the soldiers issued a curfew by shooting a few rounds into the air and ordering everyone to "get inside and stay low to the ground." That night Musa told no stories and Moriba didn't play marbles with the other boys. We quietly sat against the wall listening to the rapid bursts of gunfire in the distance. Just before the last hours of night, the moon sailed through the clouds, showing its face through the open window of the building before it was driven away by a cockcrow.

That morning didn't come just with sunrise; it brought with it soldiers, the few who were able to make it back to the village. Their well-polished boots were drenched in dirt and they sat away from each other, clinging tightly to their guns, as if those were the only things that comforted them. One soldier, who sat on a cement brick underneath the kitchen, bowed his head in his hands and rocked his body. He got up and walked around the village and returned to sit on the brick again. He did this over and over throughout the day. Lieutenant Jabati was on the radio, and at some point he threw it against the wall and walked into his room. We civilians didn't speak among ourselves during that day. We only watched the madness unfold in some of the soldiers.

At midday a group of over twenty soldiers arrived in the village. The lieutenant was surprised and delighted when he saw them, but he quickly hid his emotions. The soldiers prepared themselves and left for war. There was nothing to hide anymore; we knew the war was near.

Soon after the soldiers left, we began hearing gunshots closer to the village. The soldiers who guarded the village ordered everyone inside. The gunfight went on into the evening, interrupting the songs of birds and the chants of crickets. At night soldiers came running to the village for ammunition and a quick respite. Wounded soldiers were brought back only to die by lamplit surgery. The soldiers never brought back their dead colleagues. Prisoners were lined up and shot in the head.

These things went on for many days, and each time the soldiers went to the front lines, few returned. Those left behind became restless and started shooting civilians who were on their way to latrines at night. The lieutenant asked his men to gather everyone at the square.

"In the forest there are men waiting to destroy all of our lives. We have fought them as best as we can, but there are too many of them. They are all around the village." The lieutenant made a circle in the air with his hands. "They won't give up until they capture this village. They want our food and ammunition." He paused, and slowly continued: "Some of you are here because they have killed your parents or families, others because this is a safe place to be. Well, it is not that safe anymore. That is why we need strong men and boys to help us fight these guys, so that we can keep this village safe. If you do not want to fight or help, that is fine. But you will not have rations and will not stay in this village. You are free to leave, because we only want people here who can help cook, prepare ammunition, and fight. There are enough women to run the kitchen, so we need the help of able boys and men to fight these rebels. This is your time to revenge the deaths of your families and to make sure more children do not lose their families." He took a deep breath. "Tomorrow morning you must all line up here, and we will select people for various tasks that have to be carried out." He left the square, followed by his men.

We stood in silence for a while and slowly started walking to our respective sleeping places, as the curfew was approaching. Inside, Jumah, Alhaji, Kanei, Moriba, Musa, and I quietly discussed what we were going to do.

"The rebels will kill anyone from this village because they will consider us their enemy, spies, or that we have sided with the other side of the war. That is what the staff sergeant said," Alhaji said, explaining the dilemma we faced. The rest of the boys, who were lying on their mats, got up and joined us as Alhaji continued: "It is better to stay here for now." He sighed. We had no choice. Leaving the village was as good as being dead.

"Attention. This is an order from the lieutenant. Everyone must gather at the square immediately." A soldier spoke into a megaphone. Before he had finished his last word, the square was filled. Everyone had waited for this moment that would determine what we were going to do for our safety. Before the announcement, I sat with my friends near the window in the kitchen. Their faces were blank; they showed no emotion, but their eyes looked pale with sorrow. I tried to make eye contact with each of them, but they all looked away. I tried to eat my breakfast, but fear had taken away my appetite.

As we found spots in the back of the crowd, gunshots filled the air, then faded to a silence even more unbearable than the reports.

The lieutenant stood on several bricks so that he could be high enough to be seen by all. He let silence settle in our bones, then waved his hands to some soldiers who brought before us two bodies—a man and a young boy who had lived in the village. The blood that soaked their clothes was still fresh and their eyes were open. People turned their heads away, and little children and babies began to cry. The lieutenant cleared his throat and started speaking in the midst of the cries, which eventually ceased as he went on.

"I am sorry to show you these gruesome bodies, especially with your children present. But then again, all of us here have seen death or even shaken hands with it." He turned to the bodies and continued softly: "This man and this child decided to leave this morning even though I had told them it was dangerous. The man insisted that he didn't want to be a part of our war, so I gave him his wish and let him go. Look at what happened. The rebels shot them in the clearing. My men brought them back, and I decided to show you, so that you can fully understand the situation we are in." The lieutenant went on for almost an hour, describing how rebels had cut off the heads of some people's family members and made them watch, burned entire villages along with their inhabitants, forced sons to have intercourse with their mothers, hacked newly born babies in half because they cried too much, cut open pregnant women's stomachs, took the babies out, and killed them . . . The lieutenant spat on the ground and continued on, until he was sure that he had mentioned all the ways the rebels had hurt every person in the gathering.

"They have lost everything that makes them human. They do not deserve to live. That is why we must kill every single one of them. Think of it as destroying a great evil. It is the highest service you can perform for your country." The lieutenant pulled out his pistol and fired two shots into the air. People began shouting, "We must kill them all. We must make sure they never walk this earth again." All of us hated the rebels, and we were more than determined to stop them from capturing the village. Everyone's face had begun to sadden and grow tense. The aura in the village rapidly changed after the speech. The morning sun had disappeared and the day became gloomy. It seemed as if the sky were going to break and fall on the earth. I was furious and afraid, and so were my friends. Jumah looked toward the forest with his hands behind his back, Moriba was holding his head, Kanei stared at the ground, Musa wrapped his hands around himself, Alhaji covered his eyes with his left hand, and I stood akimbo to stop my legs from shaking. All women and girls were asked to report to the kitchen; men and boys to the ammunition depot, where the soldiers watched their movies and smoked marijuana.

As we walked toward the building, a soldier who carried a G3 weapon came out and stood at the doorway. He smiled at us, lifted his gun, and fired several rounds toward the sky. We dropped to the ground, and he laughed at us as he went back inside. We walked through the door and came upon the tents inside the building. The building was roofless except for the tarpaulin that covered the boxes of ammunition and guns stacked against the wall; and in the only common space, a huge television screen sat on top of a dilapidated drum. A few meters away from the television stood a generator, along with gallons of gasoline. The soldiers came out of their tents as the staff sergeant led us to the back of the house, where none of us had been before. There were more than thirty boys there, two of whom, Sheku and Josiah, were seven and eleven years old. The rest of us were between the ages of thirteen and sixteen, except Kanei, who was now seventeen.

A soldier wearing civilian clothes, with a whistle around his neck, stepped up to a rack of AK-47s and handed one to each of us. When the soldier stood in front of me, I avoided eye contact, so he straightened my head until my eyes met his. He gave me the gun. I held it in my trembling hand. He then added the magazine, and I shook even more. "It seems that all of you have two things in common," the soldier said after he had finished testing all of us. "You are afraid of looking a man in the eye and afraid of holding a gun. Your hands tremble as if the gun is pointed at your head." He walked up and down the line for a bit and continued: "This gun"—he held the AK-47 high up—"will soon belong to you, so you better learn not to be afraid of it. That is all for today."

That night I stood at the entrance of my tent for a while, hoping my friends would come out to talk, but no one did. Alhaji stepped out and looked in my direction for a few minutes, but he then turned and just stared at the ground. I was about to walk toward him when he re-entered his tent. I inhaled the cool night breeze, which brought with it the scent of marijuana. I sighed, went back into my tent, and sat on the tarp all night unable to sleep. I just sat with my head in my hands, thoughtless. It was the first night that I was awake alone without having a migraine. As I began to ponder why this was the case, a cock started crowing, though it was still dark outside. The confused cock crowed throughout the night until morning finally arrived.

My two tent companions, Sheku and Josiah, the two youngest boys, were still sleeping when the bell rang at 6:00 a.m. for us to rise for training. "Come on, let's go." I tried to wake them with a gentle shake. They just rolled over on their sides and continued sleeping. I had to drag them off the mat by their legs and slap them until they woke up. The soldiers were already going from tent to tent dragging out those who were still asleep and splashing buckets of water on them.

We met at the training ground and new *crapes* were distributed, along with army shorts and T-shirts that were of all colors. Some people got Adidas and others Nikes. I got a black Reebok Pump and was happier about my new *crapes* than anything else that was going on. I took off my old pants, which contained the rap cassettes. As I was putting on my new army shorts, a soldier took my old pants and threw them into a blazing fire that had been set to burn our old belongings. I ran toward the fire, but the cassettes had already started to melt. Tears formed in my eyes, and my lips shook as I turned away.

After we had put on the new attire, we formed a horizontal line with legs apart and hands straight down at our sides. As we stood waiting, some of the soldiers returned from the front line and reloaded their guns and side packs with ammunition. Some had blood on their uniforms and faces, which they didn't seem to notice or simply ignored. They quickly ate breakfast and were on their way back to where they didn't look as if they wanted to return. Each soldier stood against the wall, took several deep breaths with his eyes closed, and gripped his gun tightly before beginning to run back toward the clearing.

Sheku and Josiah stood next to me as if sharing a tent with them meant that I had become their big brother. They watched me during the exercise and followed what I did instead of the soldier who had introduced himself as Corporal Gadafi. He was a young fellow, younger than the lieutenant and the staff sergeant, but he was bald and his countenance made him look much older. He had an intense face that looked, even smiling, as if he were chewing something sour.

First we ran around the building for a few minutes, and then we began to learn how to crawl in the bushes nearby. Corporal Gadafi would hold his fist up, and when he brought it down, we fell into the bushes and crawled quickly, without producing much sound, until we reached a designated tree. Then we immediately got up and crouched to take cover behind other trees. Afterward, we would run back to the training ground. The corporal didn't say much during the initial stage of training. All he said was "Not bad," "Terrible," and "Faster." He mostly used hand gestures, which he said was the only thing that would be used once we were out there. He would point to the clearing, where "words could cost you a bullet in the head." He would then smile drily and widen his eyes for us to laugh with him. After we had done the running, crawling, and crouching many times, we were allowed to have some bread and custard. The corporal gave us one minute to get the food and eat it. Whatever we hadn't eaten was taken away at the end of sixty seconds. None of us was able to finish eating on the first day, but within a week we could eat any food in a minute. It was the only part of the training that we mastered.

After the late breakfast, we lined up facing the corporal, who handed us AK-47s. When it was my turn, he looked at me intensely, as if he was trying to tell me that he was giving me something worth cherishing. He poked my chest with his finger and walked around me. When he came back to the front, he stared at me some more, his red eyes and dark face twitching. He bared his teeth as if he were preparing to attack, and my legs began to shake, when he started to smile. Before I could smile with him, he had stopped, and the veins on his forehead stood up. Still looking straight at me, he reached into a wooden crate and pulled out the gun. He took out the magazine and handed me the AK with two hands. I hesitated for a bit, but he pushed the gun against my chest. With trembling hands I took the gun, saluted him, and ran to the back of the line, still holding the gun but afraid to look at it. I had never held a gun that long before and it frightened me. The closest thing to it had been a toy gun made out of bamboo when I was seven. My playmates and I carved them and played war games in the coffee farms and unfinished buildings at my grandmother's village. *Paw paw*, we would go, and whoever did it first would announce to the rest whom he had killed.

We continued the training exercises we had been doing earlier in the morning, but this time we carried with us AK-47s that didn't contain any ammunition. We crawled with the guns on our backs, in our hands, and ran around the building with them. The guns were a little heavy for Sheku and Josiah, who kept dropping them and picking them up as we went along. We broke for a minute lunch and began a different drill. We were taken to a nearby banana farm, where we practiced stabbing the banana trees with bayonets. "Visualize the banana tree as the enemy, the rebels who killed your parents, your family, and those who are responsible for everything that has happened to you," the corporal screamed. "Is that how you stab someone who had killed your family?" he asked. "This is how I would do it." He took out his bayonet and started shouting and stabbing the banana tree. "I first stab him in the stomach, then the neck, then his heart, and I will cut it out, show it to him, and then pluck his eyes out. Remember, he probably killed your parents worse. Continue." He wiped his knife with banana leaves. When he said this, we all got angry and drove our knives in and out of the banana trees until they fell to the ground. "Good," he said, nodding and pondering something that made him smile longer than usual. Over and over in our training he would say that same sentence: *Visualize the enemy, the rebels who killed your parents, your family, and those who are responsible for everything that has happened to you.*

That afternoon we learned how to put the magazine into the gun and other such basics. Ignore the safety pin, they said, it will only slow you down. That evening we learned to fire our guns, aiming at plywood boards mounted in the branches of tiny trees at the edge of the forest. Sheku and Josiah weren't strong enough to raise their weapons, so the corporal gave them each a high stool to keep the weapons from falling. At the end of the shooting exercise, we were taught how to dismantle our guns and oil them, because the AKs were so old that they would misfire randomly and sometimes would stop working altogether. That night, as soon as we got under the tent, my tent companions passed out. Instead of smiling in their sleep, Sheku went *"Paw*

paw, boom," and Josiah went, "One, two," the numbers we had recited as we stabbed the banana trees. But even though I was exhausted, I couldn't sleep. My ears rang with the gun sounds, my body ached, and my index finger was sore. There had been no time to think all day, but now I could. I could become angry, yes, begin to visualize scenarios of shooting or stabbing a rebel. "The rebels are responsible for everything that has happened to you." I imagined capturing several rebels at once, locking them inside a house, sprinkling gasoline on it, and tossing a match. We watch it burn and I laugh.

I was distracted by the humming of a boy named Lansana. He was three tents down from me and he sometimes hummed melodies of songs I had never heard until he fell asleep. He started doing this after our first shooting exercise. His voice would echo in the dark forest, and whenever he stopped, the night got quieter.

13

IT MUST HAVE BEEN a Sunday morning when the corporal told us to take the day off training. He tapped the palm of his hand with the flat edge of his bayonet. "If you are religious, I mean a Christian, worship your Lord today, because you might not have another chance. Dismissed."

We went to the square wearing our army shorts and the *crapes* that had been given to us. We started a soccer game, and as we played, the lieutenant came out to sit on the verandah of his house. We stopped the game and saluted him. "Carry on with the game. Right now I want to see my soldiers play soccer." He sat on the stoop and began reading *Julius Caesar*.

When we were done with soccer, we decided to go to the river for a swim. It was a sunny day, and as we ran down to the river, I felt the cool breeze drying the sweat on my body. We played swimming games for a few minutes, then divided into two teams for an ambush game. The first group to capture all the members of the other group would win.

"Let's go, soldiers, the holiday is over," the corporal called out from the banks of the river. We stopped our playing and followed him to the village. As we jogged to catch up with him, we jokingly tripped and pushed each other into the bushes.

At the village we were asked to quickly service our AK-47s. As we cleaned our guns, backpacks and waist packs were distributed among us. Two crates of ammunition were set out, one containing loaded magazines, the other loose bullets. The corporal commanded us to take as much ammunition as we could carry. "Don't take too much, though. We want you to be able to run fast," he said. As I loaded my backpack and waist pack, I looked up and saw that some of the older soldiers were doing the same. My hand began to shake and my heart beat faster. All the other boys, except for Alhaji, were having fun, because they thought they were gearing up for more drills, but I knew we weren't going for training, and Alhaji leaned on the wall of the building clutching his gun like a mother would hold her baby. He knew it, too.

"Stand up on your feet, soldiers," the corporal said. He had left us briefly to change. He was fully dressed in army uniform and carried a backpack and a waist pack full of ammunition. He held a G3 weapon and his helmet under his arms. We stood in line for inspection. All of the boys wore army shorts and green T-shirts. The corporal handed us green head ties and said, "If you see anyone without a head tie of this color or a helmet like mine, shoot him." He screamed the last two words. Now it was clear to all that we weren't going for training. As we tied our head cloths, Sheku, standing next to me, fell backward. He had taken too much ammunition. The corporal emptied some of the magazines from his backpack and stood him up. Sheku's forehead was sweating and his lips trembled. The corporal patted him on the head and continued talking. "The other men"—he pointed to the older soldiers— "will carry spare boxes of ammunition, so do not overload yourselves. Now relax, we will be on our way in a few minutes."

The corporal walked away. We sat down on the ground, and everyone seemed to wander into their own thoughts. The daily birdsongs were gone, replaced now by the raising of firing levers as the older soldiers readied themselves. Sheku and Josiah sat next to me, their eyes watery and dull. All I could do was rub their heads to assure them it might be okay. I got up and walked over to Alhaji and the rest of my friends. We made a pact that no matter what, we would try and stay together.

A young soldier came by with a plastic bag full of some kind of tablets. They looked like capsules, but they were plain white. He handed them to each of us with a cup of water. "The corporal said it will boost your energy," the soldier announced with a secretive smile on his face. As soon as we had taken the tablets, it was time to leave. The adult soldiers led the way. Some carried ammunition boxes, the length of two cement bricks, between them, and others had semi-automatic machine guns and RPGs. I held my AK-47 with my right hand, its mouth pointing to the ground. I had attached an extra magazine with adhesive tape to the one inside the gun. I had my bayonet on my left hip and some magazines and loose bullets in my side pack. In my backpack I had more magazines and loose bullets. Josiah and Sheku dragged the tip of their guns, as they still weren't strong enough to carry them and the guns were taller than they were. We were supposed to come back that evening, so we carried no food or water. "There are a lot of streams in the forest," the lieutenant had said, walking away, leaving the corporal to finish what he had started. "It is better to carry more ammunition than food and water. Because with more ammo, we will be able to find water and food, but with more water and food, we will not make it to the end of the day," the corporal explained.

The women and older people in the village stood on their verandahs and watched as we were led away by the adult soldiers into the clearing toward the forest. A baby cried uncontrollably in his mother's arms, as if he knew what lay ahead of us. The sun's brightness painted our shadows on the ground.

I have never been so afraid to go anywhere in my life as I was that day. Even the scuttle of a lizard frightened my entire being. A slight breeze blew and it went through my brain with a sharp swoop that made me grit my teeth in pain. Tears had begun to form in my eyes, but I struggled to hide them and gripped my gun for comfort.

We walked into the arms of the forest, holding our guns as if they were the only thing that gave us strength. We exhaled quietly, afraid that our own breathing could cause our death. The lieutenant led the line that I was in. He raised his fist in the air and we stopped moving. Then he slowly brought it down and we sat on one heel, our eyes surveying the forest. I wanted to turn around to see my friends' faces, but I couldn't. We began to move swiftly among the bushes until we came to the edge of a swamp, where we formed an ambush, aiming our guns into the swamp. We lay flat on our stomachs and waited. I was lying next to Josiah. Then there was Sheku and an adult soldier between myself, Jumah, and Musa. I looked around to see if I could catch their eyes, but they were concentrated on the invisible target in the swamp. The top of my eyes began to ache and the pain slowly rose up to my head. My ears became warm and tears were running down my cheeks, even though I wasn't crying. The veins on my arms stood out and I could feel them pulsating as if they had begun to breathe of their own accord. We waited in the quiet, as hunters do, our fingers gently caressing the triggers. The silence tormented me.

The short trees in the swamp began to shake as the rebels made their way through them. They weren't yet visible, but the lieutenant had passed the word down through a whisper that was relayed like a domino effect: "Fire on my command." As we watched, a group of men dressed in civilian clothes emerged from under the tiny bushes. They waved their hands and more fighters came out. Some were boys, as young as we were. They sat together in line, waving their hands, planning a strategy. The lieutenant ordered an RPG to be fired, but the commander of the rebels heard it as it whooshed its way out of the forest. "Retreat!" he told his men, and the grenade's blast got only a few men, whose split bodies flew in the air. The explosion was followed by an exchange of fire from both sides. I lay there with my gun pointed in front of me, unable to shoot. My index finger had become numb. The forest had begun to spin. I felt as if the ground had turned upside down and I was going to fall off, so I clutched the base of a tree with one hand. I couldn't think, but I could hear the sounds of the guns far away in the distance and the cries of people dying in pain. I had begun to fall into some sort of nightmare. A splash of blood hit my face. In my reverie I had opened my mouth a bit, so I tasted some of the blood. As I spat it out and wiped it off my face, I saw the soldier it had come from. Blood poured out of the bullet holes in him like water rushing through newly opened tributaries. His eyes were wide open; he still held his gun. My eyes were fixed on him when I heard Josiah scream. He cried for his mother in the most painfully piercing voice that I had ever heard. It vibrated inside my head to the point that I felt my brain had shaken loose from its anchor.

The sun showed flashes of the tips of guns and bullets traveling toward us. Bodies had begun to pile on top of each other near a short palm tree, where fronds dripped blood. I searched for Josiah. An RPG had tossed his tiny body off the ground and he had landed on a tree stump. He wiggled his legs as his cry gradually came to an end. There was blood everywhere. It seemed as if bullets were falling into the forest from all angles. I crawled to Josiah and looked into his eyes. There were tears in them and his lips were shaking, but he could not speak. As I watched him, the water in his eyes was replaced with blood that quickly turned his brown eyes into red. He reached for my shoulder as if he wanted to hold it and pull himself up. But midway, he stopped moving. The gunshots faded in my head, and it was as if my heart had stopped and the whole world had come to a standstill. I covered his eyes with my fingers and pulled him from the tree stump. His backbone had been shattered. I placed him flat on the ground and picked up my gun. I did not realize that I had stood up to take Josiah off the tree stump. I felt someone tugging at my foot. It was the corporal; he was saying something that I couldn't understand. His mouth moved and he looked terrified. He pulled me down, and as I hit the ground, I felt my brain shaking in my skull again and my deafness disappeared. "Get down," he was screaming. "Shoot," he said, as he crawled away from me to resume his position. As I looked to where he lay, my eyes caught Musa, whose head was covered with blood. His hands looked too relaxed. I turned toward the swamp, where there were gunmen running, trying to cross over. My face, my hands, my shirt and gun were covered with blood. I raised my gun and pulled the trigger, and I killed a man. Suddenly, as if someone was shooting them inside my brain, all the massacres I had seen since the day I was touched by war began flashing in my head. Every time I stopped shooting to change magazines and saw my two young lifeless friends, I angrily pointed my gun into the swamp and killed more people. I shot everything that moved, until we were ordered to retreat because we needed another strategy.

We took the guns and ammunition off the bodies of my friends and left them there in the forest, which had taken on a life of its own, as if it had trapped the souls that had departed from the dead. The branches of the trees looked as if they were holding hands and bowing their heads in prayer. We crouched into the forest and formed another ambush a few meters away from our initial position. Once again, we waited. It was between evening and nighttime. One lonely cricket tried to start singing, but none of its companions joined in, so it stopped to let silence bring night. I lay next to the corporal, whose eyes were redder than normal. He ignored my stare. We heard footsteps on the dried grasses and immediately took aim. A group of gunmen and boys emerged from under the bushes, crouched, and took quick cover behind trees. As they got closer, we opened fire, dropping those who stood in front. The rest we chased into the swamp, where we lost them. There, crabs had already begun feasting on the eyes of the dead. Limbs and fragmented skulls lay on top of the bog, and the water in the swamp had been replaced by blood. We flipped the bodies over and took their ammunition and guns.

I was not afraid of these lifeless bodies. I despised them and kicked them to flip them. I found a G3, some ammunition, and a handgun that the corporal kept for himself. I noticed that most of the dead gunmen and boys wore lots of jewelry on their necks and wrists. Some even wore more than five gold watches on one wrist. One boy, whose uncombed hair was now soaked with blood, wore a Tupac Shakur T-shirt that said: "All eyes on me." We lost a few adult soldiers on our side and my friends Musa and Josiah. Musa, the storyteller, was gone. There was no one around to tell us stories and make us laugh at times when we needed it. And Josiah—if only I had let him continue sleeping on the first day of training, perhaps he wouldn't have gone to the front line in the first place.

We arrived in the village with nightfall and sat against the walls of the army house. It was quiet, and as if we were afraid of silence, we began cleaning the blood off our guns and the ones we had brought with us, cleaning and oiling their chambers. We shot the weapons into the air to test their effectiveness. I went for supper that night, but was unable to eat. I only drank water and felt nothing. As I walked back to my tent, I stumbled into a cement wall. My knee bled, but I didn't feel a thing. I lay on my back in the tent with my AK-47 on my chest and the G3 I had brought with me leaning on the peg of the tent. Nothing happened in my head. It was void, and I stared at the roof of the tent until I was miraculously able to doze off. I had a dream that I was picking up Josiah from the tree stump and a gunman stood on top of me. He placed his gun on my forehead. I immediately woke up from my dream and began shooting inside the tent, until the thirty rounds in the magazine were finished. The corporal and the lieutenant came in afterward and took me outside. I was sweating, and they threw water on my face and gave me a few more of the white capsules. I stayed up all night and couldn't sleep for a week. We went out two more times that week and I had no problem shooting my gun.

14

THE SHARP ACHES IN MY HEAD, or what I later came to know as migraines, stopped as my daily activities were replaced with more soldierly things. In the daytime, instead of playing soccer in the village square, I took turns at the guarding posts around the village, smoking marijuana and sniffing *brown brown*, cocaine mixed with gunpowder, which was always spread out on the table, and of course taking more of the white capsules, as I had become addicted to them. They gave me a lot of energy. The first time I took all these drugs at the same time, I began to perspire so much that I took off all my clothes. My body shook, my sight became blurred, and I lost my hearing for several minutes. I walked around the village aimlessly, as I felt restless because I simultaneously felt a tremendous rush of energy and numbness. But after several doses of these drugs, all I felt was numbness to everything and so much energy that I couldn't sleep for weeks. We watched movies at night. War movies, *Rambo: First Blood, Rambo II, Commando*, and so on, with the aid of a generator or sometimes a car battery. We all wanted to be like Rambo; we couldn't wait to implement his techniques.

When we ran out of food, drugs, ammunition, and gasoline to

watch war films, we raided rebel camps, in towns, villages, and forests. We also attacked civilian villages to capture recruits and whatever else we could find.

"We have good news from our informants. We are moving out in five minutes to kill some rebels and take their supplies, which really belong to us," the lieutenant would announce. His face evinced confidence; his smiles disappeared before they were completed. We tied our heads with the green cloths that distinguished us from the rebels, and we boys led the way. There were no maps and no questions asked. We were simply told to follow the path until we received instructions on what to do next. We walked for long hours and stopped only to eat sardines and corned beef with *gari*, sniff cocaine, *brown brown*, and take some white capsules. The combination of these drugs gave us a lot of energy and made us fierce. The idea of death didn't cross my mind at all and killing had become as easy as drinking water. My mind had not only snapped during the first killing, it had also stopped making remorseful records, or so it seemed. After we ate and did drugs, we would guard the perimeter while the adults rested for a bit. I shared a post with Alhaji, and we would time each other on how fast we could take out a magazine and replace it.

"Sometime I am going to take on a whole village by myself, just like Rambo," Alhaji told me, smiling at the new goal he had set for himself.

"I'd like to have some bazookas of my own, like the ones in *Commando*. That would be beautiful," I said, and we laughed.

Before we got to a rebel camp, we would deviate from the path and walk inside the forest. Once the camp was in sight, we would surround it and wait for the lieutenant's command. The rebels roamed about; some sat against walls, dozing off, and others, boys as young as we, stood at guard posts passing around marijuana. Whenever I looked at rebels during raids, I got angrier, because they looked like the rebels who played cards in the ruins of the village where I had lost my family. So when the lieutenant gave orders, I shot as many as I could, but I didn't feel better. After every gunfight we would enter the rebel camp, killing those we had wounded. We would then search the houses and gather gallons of gasoline, enormous amounts of marijuana and co-caine, bales of clothes, *crapes*, watches, rice, dried fish, salt, *gari*, and many other things. We rounded up the civilians—men, women, boys, and young girls—hiding in the huts and houses, and made them carry our loot back to the base.

On one of these raids, we had captured a few rebels after a long gunfight and a lot of civilian casualties. We undressed the prisoners and tied them until their chests were tight as drums.

"Where did you get all this ammunition from?" the corporal asked one of the prisoners, a man with an almost dreadlocked beard. He spat at the corporal's face, and the corporal immediately shot him in the head at close range. He fell onto the ground and blood slowly leaked out of his head. We cheered in admiration of the corporal's fierceness and saluted him as he walked by. Suddenly Lansana, one of the boys, was shot in the chest and head by a rebel hiding in the bushes. We dispersed around the village in search of the shooter. When the young muscular rebel was captured, the lieutenant slit his neck with his bayonet. The rebel ran up and down the village before he fell to the ground and stopped moving. We cheered again, raising our guns in the air, shouting and whistling.

"If anyone starts any funny business, shoot him." The lieutenant eyed the prisoners. We set the thatched roofs on fire and left, taking the prisoners with us. The flames on the thatched roofs waved us off as they danced with the afternoon breeze, swaying as if in agony.

"We"—the lieutenant pointed to us—"are here to protect you and will do all we can to make sure nothing happens to you." He pointed to the civilians.

"Our job is a serious one and we have the most capable soldiers, who will do anything to defend this country. We are not like the rebels, those riffraffs who kill people for no reason. We kill them for the good and betterment of this country. So respect all these men"—he pointed to us again—"for offering their services." The lieutenant went on and on with his speech, which was a combination of instilling in the civilians that what we were doing was right and boosting the morale of his men, including us, the boys. I stood there holding my gun and felt special because I was part of something that took me seriously and I was not running from anyone anymore. I had my gun now, and as the corporal always said, "This gun is your source of power in these times. It will protect you and provide you all you need, if you know how to use it well."

I cannot remember what prompted the lieutenant to make this speech. A lot of things were done with no reason or explanation. Sometimes we were asked to leave for war in the middle of a movie. We would come back hours later after killing many people and continue the movie as if we had just returned from intermission. We were always either at the front lines, watching a war movie, or doing drugs. There was no time to be alone or to think. When we conversed with each other, we talked only about the war movies and how impressed we were with the way either the lieutenant, the corporal, or one of us had killed someone. It was as if nothing else existed outside our reality.

The morning after the lieutenant's speech, we proceeded to practice killing the prisoners the way the lieutenant had done it. There were five prisoners and many eager participants. So the corporal chose a few of us. He picked Kanei, three other boys, and me for the killing exhibition. The five men were lined up in front of us on the training ground with their hands tied. We were supposed to slice their throats on the corporal's command. The person whose prisoner died quickest would win the contest. We had our bayonets out and were supposed to look in the faces of the prisoners as we took them out of this world. I had already begun staring at my prisoner. His face was swollen from the beating he had received, and his eyes looked as if they were watching something behind me. His jaws were the only tense part of his facial expression; everything else seemed calm. I didn't feel a thing for him, didn't think that much about what I was doing. I just waited for the corporal's order. The prisoner was simply another rebel who was responsible for the death of my family, as I had come to truly believe.

The corporal gave the signal with a pistol shot and I grabbed the man's head and slit his throat in one fluid motion. His Adam's apple made way for the sharp knife, and I turned the bayonet on its zigzag edge as I brought it out. His eyes rolled up and they looked me straight in the eye before they suddenly stopped in a frightful glance, as if caught by surprise. The prisoner leaned his weight on me as he gave out his last breath. I dropped him on the ground and wiped my bayonet on him. I reported to the corporal, who was holding a timer. The bodies of the other prisoners fought in the arms of the other boys, and some continued to shake on the ground for a while. I was proclaimed the winner, and Kanei came second. The boys and the other soldiers who were the audience clapped as if I had just fulfilled one of life's greatest achievements. I was given the rank of junior lieutenant and Kanei was given junior sergeant. We celebrated that day's achievement with more drugs and more war movies.

I had a tent to myself, which I never slept in because sleep never came to me. Sometimes late in the night, the quiet wind brought to my ears the humming of Lansana. It seemed as if the trees whispered the tunes of the songs he had sung. I would listen for a bit and then fire a few rounds into the night, driving the humming away.

15

THE VILLAGES THAT WE CAPTURED and turned into our bases as we went along and the forests that we slept in became my home. My squad was my family, my gun was my provider and protector, and my rule was to kill or be killed. The extent of my thoughts didn't go much beyond that. We had been fighting for over two years, and killing had become a daily activity. I felt no pity for anyone. My childhood had gone by without my knowing, and it seemed as if my heart had frozen. I knew that day and night came and went because of the presence of the moon and the sun, but I had no idea whether it was a Sunday or a Friday.

In my head my life was normal. But everything began to change in the last weeks of January 1996. I was fifteen.

I left one morning with twenty members of my squad for Bauya, a small town a day's walk south of us, to get ammunition. My friends Alhaji and Kanei came, too. We were excited to see Jumah, who was now stationed there. We wanted to hear his war stories, hear how many people he had killed. I was also looking forward to seeing the lieutenant. I hoped we might find some time to talk about Shakespeare.

We walked in two lines on the sides of a dusty path, looking into the dense bushes with our bloodshot eyes. We arrived at the outskirts of Bauya just before sunset and waited in the bushes as our commander went ahead to make sure our colleagues wouldn't shoot at us. We sat against trees and watched the path. The commander returned after several minutes and motioned for us to move into town. I hoisted my gun on my shoulder and walked next to Kanei and Alhaji as we entered the base. The cement houses in the town were bigger than the ones I had seen in other villages, and everywhere we looked were unfamiliar faces. We nodded to acknowledge other soldiers as we walked around town looking for Jumah. We found him sitting in a hammock on the verandah of a cement house that faced the forest. There was a semiautomatic machine gun next to him and he seemed lost in thought. We slowly walked up to him, but before we could scare him, he heard our footsteps and turned toward us. His face seemed to have gotten older and he had stopped nodding when he spoke. We shook hands with him and examined his gun.

"I see that you carry heavy weapons these days," Alhaji joked with him.

"Well, what can I say, I am moving up from the AKs," he replied, and we all laughed.

We told him that we would return to sit with him in a few minutes and went to load our bags with ammunition and food to take back. While we were in the ammunition house, our commander told us that the lieutenant had asked us to stay the night and that dinner was ready. I wasn't hungry, so I returned by myself to see Jumah while Kanei and Alhaji went to eat. We sat quietly for a while before he started talking.

"I am going on a raid tomorrow morning, so I might not see you before you leave." He paused, fingered the side of the machine gun, and continued: "I killed the owner of this gun in our last raid. He took out a lot of us before I could get him. Since then I have used it to do some damage myself." He chuckled, and we high-fived each other and laughed. Immediately after that, we were ordered to report for the nightly gathering in the yard at the center of town. It was a social event for commanders to mingle with everyone else. Jumah picked up his gun and put his arm around my shoulder as we walked to the yard. Alhaji and Kanei were there; they had already started smoking. Lieutenant Jabati was present, too, and he was a little jovial that night. Most of his colleagues, Staff Sergeant Mansaray and Corporal Gadafi, had died, but the lieutenant had miraculously managed to stay alive unscarred. He had also been able to replace his dead colleagues with other men who were fierce and disciplined. I wanted to talk to the lieutenant about Shakespeare, but he was busy going about the gathering, shaking everyone's hand. When he finally stood in front of me, he held my hand tight and said, "Macbeth shall never vanquished be until great Birnam Wood to high Dunsinane hill shall come against him." He nodded at me and said loudly to everyone, "I shall take leave of you fine gentlemen." He bowed and waved as he left. We raised our guns in the air and cheered. After the lieutenant had gone, we began singing the national anthem, "*High we exalt thee, realm of the free, great is the love we have for thee . . .*" and marching, smoking and sniffing the cocaine and *brown brown* that was in abundance at Bauya. We chatted all night, mostly about how good the drugs were.

Before morning, Jumah and a few others left for their raid. Alhaji, Kanei, and I shook hands with him and promised that we would catch up more on our next visit. Jumah smiled, clutched his machine gun, and went running into the darkness.

A few hours later a truck came to the village. Four men dressed in clean blue jeans and white T-shirts that said UNICEF on them in big blue letters jumped out. One of them was a white man and another was also light-skinned, maybe Lebanese. The other two were nationals, one with tribal marks on his cheeks, the other with marks on his hands just like the one my grandfather gave me to protect me from snakebite. The men were all too clean to have been in the war. They were shown to the lieutenant's house. He had been expecting them. As they sat talking on the verandah, we watched them from under the mango tree, where we sat cleaning our guns. After a while, the lieutenant shook hands with the two foreigners and he called over the private who was guarding the meeting. The private ran toward us and told us to form a line. He went around the town gathering all the boys, exclaiming: "This is an order from the lieutenant!" We were accustomed to taking orders and did what we were told. We formed a horizontal line and waited.

The lieutenant stood before us and we saluted him, expecting to hear about our next raid on a rebel camp. "Stand at ease, boys," he said. He slowly walked along the line, the visitors a few paces behind him, smiling.

"When I point at you, fall out and form a line by the private. Understand." The lieutenant gave his orders from the far end of the line. "Yes, sir," we shouted, and saluted. The smiles on the visitors' faces disappeared. "At ease."

"You, you . . ." the lieutenant pointed as he walked down the line. When the lieutenant picked me, I stared at his face, but he ignored me and continued his selection process. Alhaji was also picked, but Kanei was left behind, maybe because he was older. Fifteen of us were chosen. The lieutenant then ordered us, "Remove your magazines, put your weapons on safety, and put them on the ground." We laid our weapons down, and the visitors, especially the two foreigners, began smiling again. "Attention. Forward march," a private ordered us, and we followed the lieutenant toward the truck the visitors had arrived in. We stopped when the lieutenant turned around and faced us. "You have been great soldiers and you all know that you are part of this brotherhood. I am very proud to have served my country with you boys. But your work here is done, and I must send you off. These men will put you in school and find you another life." That was all he said; then he smiled and walked away, asking the other soldiers to strip us of our military equipment. I hid my bayonet inside my pants and a grenade in my pocket. When one of the soldiers came to search me, I pushed him and told him that if he touched me I would kill him. He walked away and searched a boy standing next to me instead.

What was happening? Our faces followed the lieutenant as he walked to his house. Why had the lieutenant decided to give us up to these civilians? We thought that we were part of the war until the end. The squad had been our family. Now we were being taken away, just like that, without any explanation. A few soldiers gathered our weapons and others guarded us, to make sure that we didn't try to run for our guns. As we were ushered to the truck, I stared back at the verandah where the lieutenant now stood, looking in the other direction, toward the forest, his hands crossed behind his back. I still didn't know what was going on, but I was beginning to get angry, anxious. I hadn't parted with my gun since the day I became a soldier.

In the truck were three MPs—city soldiers. I could tell by how clean their uniforms and guns were. Their pants were tucked inside their boots and their shirts were tucked into their pants. Their faces weren't hardened, and their guns were so clean I assumed they hadn't fired a shot. The weapons were on safety. The MPs jumped off the truck and motioned for us to climb in. We divided ourselves onto two long benches in the truck that faced each other, and two of the men, the one with the marks on his cheeks and the Lebanese-looking foreigner, climbed in back with us. Then the three MPs swung up on the back door panel, one foot inside the truck, the other hanging out.

As the truck began to pull away from the base, I started boiling with anger, because I couldn't make sense of what was happening. Alhaji looked at me with a puzzled face. I looked at the guns the MPs carried and envied them. The men who had come to get us smiled as the truck sped along the dirt road, raising light brown dust that covered the bushes on the sides of the road. I had no idea where we were going.

We were on the road for hours. I had gotten used to walking to places and hadn't sat in a truck or been in one place idly for this long in a while. I hated it. I thought about hijacking the truck and driving it back to Bauya. But whenever I was ready to snatch a gun from the MPs, the truck slowed down at a checkpoint and the soldiers jumped off. I had forgotten about the grenade in the side pocket of my army shorts. I was restless throughout the journey and actually began to look forward to the checkpoints (there were many of them, too many) so that I could get up from the boredom of the truck. We didn't speak to each other at all. We sat quietly, except at times when I winked at Alhaji as we waited for the right moment to take the guns from the MPs and push them off the truck.

The last checkpoint we passed that day was manned by soldiers well dressed in complete army gear. The brown polished wooden panels of their AKs were shiny and new. They were city soldiers who, like the MPs who were in the truck with us, hadn't yet been to war. They had no idea, I thought, what was really happening in the bushes in the entire country.

We drove past the checkpoint, off the dusty road, and onto a busy tar street. Everywhere I looked there were cars going in every direction. I had never seen that many cars, trucks, and buses in my life. Mercedes, Toyotas, Mazdas, Chevrolets were impatiently honking, music blasting. I still didn't know where we were going, but I was sure now that we were in Freetown, Sierra Leone's capital. But I didn't know why.

It was getting dark outside. As the truck slowly rocked along the busy street, streetlights flickered on. Even the shops and kiosks were lit. I was amazed at how many lights there were without the sound of a generator. I was marveling at the glittering cityscape when the truck turned off the street and began galloping so heavily that we were all shaking as if we'd been placed on a vibrating machine. This went on for a few minutes, and then we stopped. The MPs asked us to get out of the truck and follow the four beaming men in the UNICEF shirts.

We entered a fenced compound that had several rows of houses. There were lights on in the houses and boys our age, fifteen and above, sat on the verandahs and stoops. They ignored us, as they, too, looked baffled about why they were there. The Lebanese-looking foreigner motioned for us to follow him into the house, his face glowing. It was an open hall and there were two rows of twin-size beds. He excitedly showed each of us the bed that was going to be ours and lockers that contained soap, toothpaste, toothbrush, a towel, a clean shirt, and T-shirts. The beds had pillows, clean sheets, and blankets. None of us were as interested in the things he showed us as he seemed to be. "We have a bale of new *crapes* for you. Tomorrow you will pick your size." He left us in the room and went outside, whistling a melody. We just stood there looking at the beds as if we had never seen anything like them.

"Come with me to the kitchen for some food," the Sierra Leonean man with the tribal marks said. We followed him past the curious faces of boys who had arrived before us. Their eyes were as red as ours, and even though they wore civilian clothes, they looked dirty and had intense expressions like us. I could smell the forest on them.

In the kitchen we sat on one side of the long dining table. The man went into a little room at the end of the kitchen, where he hummed a familiar song, dished out rice into many bowls, and brought them out on a tray. We took a bowl each and started eating. He went back into the little room, and by the time he returned to the table with his own bowl of food to eat with us, we had already finished. He was shocked and looked around to see if we had done something else with the food. He pulled himself together, and as he was about to take his first bite, the two happy-face foreigners walked into the dining room and asked him to come with them. He took his bowl of rice with him and followed the foreigners, who were already walking out of the kitchen. We sat quietly for a minute before Alhaji asked if anyone happened to bring some marijuana or cocaine. One of the boys had some marijuana that we passed around, but it wasn't enough. "Where can we get ourselves some good drugs in this place?" one of the boys asked.

As we pondered this question, the man who had brought us to the kitchen returned, bringing with him another group of boys, over twenty of them. "These are the new arrivals," he said to us. Turning to the new boys, he said, "I'll bring you some food, and please, take your time. There is no need to eat fast." The boys sat on the opposite side of the dining table and ate as fast as we had. The man sniffed the air and asked, "Who was smoking marijuana in here?" But no one paid him any attention, so he sat down and kept quiet. We stared at the new boys and they at us.

Alhaji broke the silence. "Where are you boys from?" he asked. The boys widened their eyes and stared at Alhaji as if he had just asked them the wrong question. One of the boys, who looked a little older and had no hair on his head, stood up, clenching his fist.

"And who the fuck are you? Do we look like we are here to answer questions for *bastar pekin lek you*?" He leaned across the table and looked down on Alhaji. Alhaji got up and pushed him. The boy fell, and when he got up, he pulled a bayonet and jumped on the table toward Alhaji. All of us stood up, ready to fight. The man screamed, "Stop it, boys!" but no one listened to him. I took out my grenade and put my fingers inside the pin.

"Do you boys want this to be your last meal, or do you want to answer his question?" I threatened the other boys.

"We are from Kono district," the boy who held the bayonet said.

"Ah, the diamond area!" Alhaji said. I was still holding the grenade.

"Did you fight in the army or for the rebels?" I sternly asked.

"Do I look like a rebel to you?" he said. "I fought for the army. The rebels burned my village and killed my parents, and you look like one of them."

"So we all fought on the same side of the war," Alhaji said, and we all sat down, still glaring at each other. Upon learning that we had all fought for the so-called army, in different parts of the country, we calmed down and talked about what bases we were from. Neither of us had ever heard of the others' squad or base or the lieutenants who were in charge of the squads. I explained to the other boys that we had arrived just a few minutes before them. They told me that they had been randomly selected, too, and asked by their commander to follow the men who visited their base. None of us knew why our commanders had let us go. We were excellent fighters and were ready to fight the war till the end. One boy was telling us that he thought the foreigners gave our commanders money in exchange for us. No one said anything to this. I still had the grenade in my hand as we conversed. Sometime during the conversation I turned to the man who had brought us to the kitchen. He was sitting at the edge of the table, shaking. His forehead perspired profusely. "Do you know why our commanders gave us up to you sissy civilians?" I asked the man, pointing the grenade at him. He put his head under the table as if I was going to throw the grenade at him. He was too nervous to answer me.

"He is a sissy civilian, let's go ask the other boys," the boy who had pulled his bayonet suggested. His name was Mambu, and I later became friends with him. We left the man, still under the kitchen table, and headed for the verandah. As we walked up the steps, we saw the three MPs sitting at the entrance of the compound, chatting and ignoring us. The two foreigners had left. We walked up to the boys sitting quietly on the verandah.

"Do you boys know why your commanders gave you up to these civilians?" Alhaji asked, and all the quiet boys stood up and turned their angry faces to him, staring silently.

"Are you boys deaf?" Alhaji continued. He turned to me: "They don't know anything."

"We do not want to be bothered by anyone," one of the boys said in a deep voice. "And we do not want to answer any questions from a civilian."

"We are not civilians," Mambu said angrily, walking toward the boy. "If anyone is a civilian, it is you boys. You are wearing civilian clothes. What kind of army person wears only civilian clothes? Did these sissy civilians who brought you here make you wear those clothes? You must be a weak soldier, then."

"We fought for the RUF; the army is the enemy. We fought for freedom, and the army killed my family and destroyed my village. I will kill any of those army bastards every time I get a chance to do so." The boy took off his shirt to fight Mambu, and on his arm was the RUF tattoo.

"They are rebels," Mambu shouted, and before he could reach for his bayonet, the boy punched him in the face. He fell, and when he

got up, his nose was bleeding. The rebel boys drew out the few bayonets they had and rushed toward us. It was war all over again. Perhaps
the naïve foreigners thought that removing us from the war would
lessen our hatred for the RUF. It hadn't crossed their minds that a
change of environment wouldn't immediately make us normal boys;
we were dangerous, and brainwashed to kill. They had just started this
process of rehabilitation, so this was one of the first lessons they had to
learn.

As the boys rushed toward us, I threw the grenade among them, but
the explosion was delayed. We leaped out from underneath the stoop
where we had taken cover and charged into the open yard, where we
began to fight. Some of us had bayonets, others didn't. A boy without
a bayonet grabbed my neck from behind. He was squeezing for the kill
and I couldn't use my bayonet effectively, so I elbowed him with all my
might until he let go of my neck. He was holding his stomach when
I turned around. I stabbed him in his foot. The bayonet stuck, so I
pulled it out with force. He fell and I began kicking him in the face.
As I went to deliver the final blow with my bayonet, someone came
from behind me and sliced my hand with his knife. It was a rebel boy,
and he was about to kick me down when he fell on his face. Alhaji had
stabbed him in the back. He pulled the knife out, and we continued
kicking the boy until he stopped moving. I wasn't sure whether he was
unconscious or dead. I didn't care. No one screamed or cried during
the fight. After all, we had been doing such things for years and were
all still on drugs.

The three MPs and the two nationals who had brought us to the
center came running into the yard a few minutes into the fight. "Stop,
stop," they yelled, pushed boys apart, and carried the wounded to the
side. It was a bad idea. We pounced on the MPs, pulled them to
the ground, and took their guns away from them. The army boys, we,
got one; the rebel boys had the other. The other MP ran away before
either group could catch him.

Mambu had the gun, and before the rebel boy who had the other
gun could switch the safety off, Mambu shot him. He fell, dropping

the gun. Other rebel boys tried to grab it, but Mambu shot each one who attempted to. He killed a few and wounded some. But the rebel boys were persistent, and finally one of them got the gun and shot two boys on our side. The second boy, who was shot at close range, stabbed the rebel boy in his stomach before he fell. The rebel boy dropped the gun and fell to the ground as well.

More MPs were running through the gate now, toward the fight. We had fought for almost twenty minutes, stabbing and slicing each other and the men who tried to part us. The MPs fired a few rounds into the air to get us to stop, but we were still fighting, so they had to part us by force. They placed some of us at gunpoint and kicked others apart. Six people were killed: two on our side and four on the rebel side; and several were wounded, including two of the men who had brought us. The military ambulances took off, wailing into the still newborn night with the dead and the wounded. Their strobe lights made me dizzy. I had a little wound on my hand. I hid it because I didn't want to be taken to the hospital and it was just a small cut. I washed the blood off, put some salt on it and tied it with a cloth. During the fight Mambu had blinded one boy by plucking out his eye with a bayonet. We later heard that the boy was taken out of the country for surgery and that his eye was to be replaced by a cat's eye or something. Following the night of the fight, we praised Mambu for his lethal behavior. I would have liked him to be in my squad, I thought.

As MPs stood guard to make sure we didn't start another fight, we, the army boys, went to the kitchen to look for food. We ate and chatted about the fight. Mambu told us that when he plucked the boy's eye out, the boy ran to punch him, but he couldn't see him, so he ran into the wall, banging his head hard, and fainted. We laughed and picked up Mambu, raising him in the air. We needed the violence to cheer us after a whole day of boring traveling and contemplation about why our superiors had let us go.

The jubilation was stopped by a group of MPs who walked into the kitchen and asked us to follow them. They had their guns pointed at us, but we laughed at them and walked outside to where military vehi-

cles waited to transport us somewhere. We were so happy to have dealt
with the rebel boys that we didn't think of attacking the MPs. Plus
there were too many of them. It seemed they had gotten the message
that we were not children to play with. Some of the MPs stood by the
vehicle holding their guns tightly and carefully eyeing us. "Maybe they
are taking us back to the front," Alhaji said, and for some reason we all
started singing the national anthem, marching to the vehicles.

But we were not taken back to the front lines; instead, they took us
to Benin Home, another rehabilitation center in Kissy Town at the
eastern outskirts of Freetown, away from the rest of the city. Benin
Home had once been called Approve School and been a government-
run juvenile center. The MPs made sure to search us thoroughly before
we entered. The blood of our victims and enemies was fresh on our
arms and clothes. The lieutenant's words still echoed in my head:
"From now on, we kill any rebel we see, no prisoners." I smiled a bit,
happy that we had taken care of the rebel boys, but I also began to
wonder again: why had we been brought here? The MPs guarded us
that night as we sat on the verandah of our halls staring into the night.
All I could think about was what was going to happen with my G3
weapon and what movie my squad was watching that night, what
good marijuana and cocaine were at their disposal. "Hey, you fellows
have any *tafe* [marijuana] for us?" Mambu asked the MPs, who ignored him. I was beginning to shake. The drugs from the previous
nights, before we were brought to the city, had begun to subside in my
system. I walked up and down on the verandah, restless in my new
environment. My head began to hurt.

16

⬥

IT WAS INFURIATING to be told what to do by civilians. Their voices, even when they called us for breakfast, enraged me so much that I would punch the wall, my locker, or anything that I was standing next to. A few days earlier, we could have decided whether they would live or die. Because of these things, we refused to do anything that we were asked to do, except eat. We had bread and tea for breakfast, rice and soup for both lunch and dinner. The assortment of soups consisted of cassava leaves, potato leaves, okra, and so forth. We were unhappy because we needed our guns and drugs.

At the end of every meal, the nurses and staff members came to talk to us about attending the scheduled medical checkups in the mini-hospital at Benin Home and the one-on-one counseling sessions in the psychosocial therapy center that we hated. As soon as they started speaking, we would throw bowls, spoons, food, and benches at them. We would chase them out of the dining hall and beat them up. One afternoon, after we had chased off the nurses and staff members, we placed a bucket over the cook's head and pushed him around the kitchen until he burned his hand on a hot boiling pot and agreed to put more milk in our tea. Because of these things, we were basically left to wander aimlessly about our new environment for the entire first week. During that same week, the drugs were wearing off. I craved cocaine and marijuana so badly that I would roll a plain sheet of paper and smoke it. Sometimes I searched in the pockets of my army shorts, which I still wore, for crumbs of marijuana or cocaine. We broke into the mini-hospital and stole some pain relievers—white tablets and off white—and red and yellow capsules. We emptied the capsules, ground the tablets, and mixed them together. But the mixture didn't give us the effect we wanted. We got more upset day by day and, as a result, resorted to more violence. In the morning, we beat up people from the neighborhood who were on their way to fetch water at a nearby pump. If we couldn't catch them, we threw stones at them. Sometimes they dropped their buckets as they ran away from us. We would laugh as we destroyed their buckets. The neighbors stopped walking near our center, as we had sent a few of them to the hospital. The staff members avoided us all the more. We began to fight each other day and night.

We would fight for hours in between meals, for no reason at all. During these fights, we destroyed most of the furniture and threw the mattresses out in the yard. We would stop to wipe the blood off our lips, arms, and legs only when the bell rang for mealtime. At night, after we had exhausted fighting, we would bring our mattresses outside in the yard and sit on them quietly until morning arrived and it was time for breakfast. Every time we returned from breakfast, the mattresses we had brought outside the previous night were back on our beds. We would angrily bring them out again in the yard, cursing whoever had taken them inside. One night, as we sat outside on the mattresses, it began to rain. We sat in the rain wiping it off our faces and listening to its sound on the tile roof and the gushing of torrents onto the ground. It rained for only about an hour, but even after it had stopped, we continued sitting outside all night on the wet sponges that were once our mattresses.

The following morning, when we returned from breakfast, the mattresses were still outside. It wasn't much of a sunny day, so they didn't dry by nighttime. We became angry and went to look for Poppay, the man in charge of storage. He was an ex-military man with a wandering eye. When we found him, we demanded dry mattresses.

"You will have to wait for the ones you left outside to dry," he said.

"We cannot allow a civilian to talk to us like that," someone said, and we all shouted in agreement and rushed at Poppay. We unleashed blows on him. One of the boys stabbed his foot and he fell down. He put his hands over his head as we kicked him relentlessly and left him lying on the floor bleeding and unconscious. We shouted in excitement as we walked back to our verandah. Gradually, we became quiet. I was angry, because I missed my squad and needed more violence.

A security guy who watched the center took Poppay to the hospital. Several days later, Poppay returned during lunchtime, limping but with a smile on his face. "It is not your fault that you did such a thing to me," he said, as he strolled through the dining hall. This made us angry, because we wanted "the civilians," as we referred to the staff members, to respect us as soldiers who were capable of severely harming them. Most of the staff members were like that; they returned smiling after we hurt them. It was as if they had made a pact not to give up on us. Their smiles made us hate them all the more.

My hands had begun to shake uncontrollably and my migraines had returned with a vengeance. It was as if a blacksmith had an anvil in my head. I would hear and feel the hammering of metal in my head, and these unbearable sharp sounds made my veins and muscles sour. I cringed and rolled around on the floor by my bed or sometimes on the verandah. No one paid any attention, as everyone was busy going through their own withdrawal stages in different ways. Alhaji, for example, punched the cement pillar of one of the buildings until his knuckles bled and his bone began to show. He was taken to the mini-hospital and put to sleep for several days so that he would stop hurting himself.

One day we decided to break the glass windows in the classrooms. I do not remember why, but instead of finding rocks to break the windows like everyone else, I punched the glass with my fist. I managed to break several panes before my hand got stuck in the glass. I drew it out and began to bleed uncontrollably. I had to go to the hospital. My plan was to steal a first-aid kit and treat myself, but the nurse was there. She made me sit on the counter as she removed pieces of glass from my skin. She twisted her face whenever she was removing a piece of glass that was buried deep in my skin. But when she looked at me, I was still. She searched my face to see if I was in pain. She was confused, but continued to gently remove the pieces of glass from my bleeding hand. I didn't feel a thing. I just wanted to stop my blood from flowing.

"This is going to hurt," the nurse said when she was about to clean the cuts.

"What is your name?" she asked as she dressed my hand. I didn't answer her.

"Come back tomorrow so that I can change the bandage. Okay?" She began to rub my head, but I pushed her hand away and walked out.

I didn't go back to the hospital the next day, but on that same day, I fainted from a migraine while I was sitting on the verandah. I woke up in bed in the hospital. The nurse was wiping my forehead with a soaked cloth. I caught her hand, pushed her away, and walked out again. I sat outside in the sun, rocking back and forth. My entire body was aching, my throat was dry, and I felt nauseated. I threw up something green and slimy, then fainted again. When I woke up hours later, the same nurse was there. She handed me a glass of water. "You can go if you want to, but I suggest that you stay in bed tonight," she said, pointing her finger at me, the way a mother would talk to a stubborn child. I took the water from her and drank it, then threw the glass against the wall. The nurse leapt from her chair. I tried to get up to leave, but was unable to sit up in bed. She smiled and walked over to my bed and injected me. She covered me with a blanket and began sweeping up the broken glass. I wanted to throw the blanket off, but I couldn't move my hands. I was getting weaker and my eyelids grew heavier.

I woke to the whispers of the nurse and someone else. I was confused, as I wasn't sure what day or time it was. I felt my head pulsating a little. "How long have I been here?" I asked the nurse, banging my hand on the side of the bed to get her attention.

"Look who's talking, and be careful with your hand," she said. When I sat up a bit, I saw that there was a soldier in the room. I thought for a minute that he was there to take me back to the front lines. But when I looked at him again, I knew he was at the hospital for other reasons. He was clearly a city soldier, well dressed and without a gun. He was a lieutenant and supposedly there to check on how we were being treated medically and psychologically, but he seemed more interested in the nurse. I was once a lieutenant, I thought, a "junior lieutenant," to be precise.

As a junior lieutenant I had been in charge of a small unit made up of boys to carry out quick missions. The lieutenant and Corporal Gadafi had selected all my remaining friends—Alhaji, Kanei, Jumah, and Moriba—to form the unit, and once again we were back together. Only this time we weren't running away from the war. We were in it and went out scouting potential villages that had food, drugs, ammunition, gasoline, and other things we needed. I would report our findings to the corporal, and then the entire squad would attack the village we had spied on, killing everyone so that we would stay alive.

On one of our scouting expeditions, we accidentally came upon a village. We had thought that the village was more than three days away, but after only a day and a half of walking, we began to smell the scent of cooking palm oil in the air. It was a beautiful day, as summer was giving us its last sunshine. We immediately got off the path and walked in the bushes toward the village. When we began to see the thatched roofs, we crawled until we were closer to the village, to be able to look at what was going on. There were a few gunmen lazily lounging about. Also, there were piles of bundles outside every house. It seemed that the rebels were getting ready to move out of the village. If we had gone back to base to get the rest of the squad, we would have missed capturing their supply of food. So we decided to attack. I gave orders for everyone to deploy around the village at strategic positions from where they could see the entire place. Alhaji and I gave the three other boys a few minutes to take their positions before we started crawling even closer to the village to initiate the attack. The two of us went back to the main path and started crawling on either side of it. We had two RPG tubes and five propelled grenades. We had gotten close enough, and I had aimed my gun at the group that I intended to start with, when Alhaji tapped me on my shoulder. He whispered that he wanted to practice his Rambo moves before we started firing. Before I said a word, Alhaji was already rubbing mud on his face, using a combination of saliva and some of the water from his backpack to wet the mud. He tied his gun to his back and took out his bayonet, rubbing his finger on the flat edge, holding it in front of his face. He began to crawl slowly under the midday sun that illuminated the village one last time before we brought darkness to it.

When Alhaji was out of sight, I aimed the RPG at the village where most of the gunmen sat, to cover him. A few minutes later, I saw him crawling and crouching behind and among houses. He would quickly sit against walls to avoid being seen. He crawled slowly behind a lazy guard basking in the sunlight with his gun on his lap. Alhaji grabbed the guard's mouth and sliced his neck with his bayonet. He did the same to a few more guards. But he had made one mistake: he didn't hide the bodies of those he had successfully killed. I was enjoying his maneuver when one of the guards, upon returning to his post, saw the body of his colleague and began running back to tell the others. I couldn't let him do that, so I shot him with my G3 and quickly released two RPGs among the gunmen.

We began exchanging fire. I didn't know where Alhaji was, but as I was shooting, he crawled toward me. I almost shot him, but recognized his dirty Rambo face. We went to work, killing everyone in sight. We didn't waste a single bullet. We had all gotten better at shooting, and our size gave us an advantage, because we could hide under the tiniest bushes and kill men who wondered where the bullets were coming from. To gain complete control of the village, Alhaji and I shot the remaining RPGs before we descended on it.

We walked around the village and killed everyone who came out of the houses and huts. Afterward, we realized that there was no one to carry the loads. We had killed everyone. So I sent Kanei and Moriba back to base to get help. They left, taking some ammunition from the dead gunmen; some of them still clung to their guns. The three of us remained in the village. Instead of sitting among the dead bodies, the bundles of food, crates of ammunition, and bags of drugs, we took cover in the nearby bushes and guarded the village. Also, we took turns going down to the village to get something to eat and some drugs. We sat quietly under the bushes and waited.

Two days later, Kanei and Moriba returned with the corporal, some soldiers, and civilians who carried the bundles of food, drugs, and ammunition back to base.

"We have enough of everything to last us for a few months. Good job, soldiers," the corporal congratulated us. We saluted him and were on our way. Because of this raid, Alhaji acquired the name "Little Rambo," and he did all he could in other raids to live up to that name. My nickname was "Green Snake," because I would situate myself in the most advantageous and sneaky position and would take out a whole village from under the tiniest shrub without being noticed. The lieutenant gave me the name. He said, "You don't look dangerous, but you are, and you blend with nature like a green snake, deceptive and deadly when you want to be." I was happy with my name, and on every raid I made sure I did as my name required.

There was a crack on the white ceiling of the room, and I could faintly hear the deep voice of the city lieutenant and the quick laughs of the nurse. I turned my head to the side and looked in their direction. The nurse had a wide smile on her face and seemed to be interested in the lieutenant's jokes. I got up and started walking out of the hospital.

"Drink a lot of water and you will be fine. Come back tomorrow night for a checkup," the nurse called after me.

"How do you like being here?" the lieutenant asked.

I looked at him with disgust and spat on the ground. He shrugged. Just another sissy city soldier, I thought as I walked back to the hall. When I got there, two boys were playing table tennis on the verandah.

Everyone seemed to be interested in what was happening. It had been more than a month and some of us had almost gone through the withdrawal stage, even though there were still instances of vomiting and collapsing at unexpected moments. These outbreaks ended, for most of us, at the end of the second month. But we were still traumatized, and now that we had time to think, the fastened mantle of our war memories slowly began to open.

Whenever I turned on the tap water, all I could see was blood gushing out. I would stare at it until it looked like water before drinking or taking a shower. Boys sometimes ran out of the hall screaming, "The rebels are coming." Other times, the younger boys sat by rocks weeping and telling us that the rocks were their dead families. Then there were those instances when we would ambush the staff members, tie them up, and interrogate them about the whereabouts of their squad, where they got their supplies of arms and ammunition, drugs, and food. It was also during this time that we were given school supplies—books, pens, and pencils—and told that we would have classes from 10:00 a.m. to 12:00 p.m. on weekdays. We made campfires with them, and the next morning another set of supplies was handed to us. We burned them again. The staff members kept resupplying the school materials. This time they didn't say, "It's not your fault," as they usually did after we had done things they considered wrong and not childlike.

One afternoon, after the staff members had set some school supplies on the verandah, Mambu suggested that we sell them. "Who will buy them? Everyone is afraid of us," some of the boys asked. "We can find a trader who wants to do business," Mambu assured the boys. We loaded the supplies in plastic bags, and six of us went to the nearest market, where we sold them to a vendor. The man was excited and told us that he would buy from us anytime. "I don't care whether you stole this; I have the money and you have the goods, we do business," the man told us as he handed Mambu a wad of cash. Mambu counted the crisp notes with a wide smile on his face. He held the bills to our noses so that we could smell them. "This is good money. I can tell," he said. We then ran back to the center to make it in time for lunch. Immediately after we were finished eating, Mambu gave each boy his share of the money. The halls became noisy as everybody talked about what they were going to do with their money. This was definitely more exciting than burning the supplies.

While some of the boys bought Coca-Cola, toffee, and other such things with their money, Mambu, Alhaji, and I planned a trip to Freetown. All we knew was that we had to take public transportation to the city center.

That morning we gulped our breakfast and left the dining hall one at a time. I pretended I was going for a checkup at the mini-hospital, Mambu went into the kitchen as if to get more food and climbed out the window, Alhaji walked toward the latrine. We didn't want the other boys to know, as we were worried that they would all come along and the staff would panic. The three of us met at the junction down by the center and stood in line, waiting for the bus.

"Have you ever been to the city?" Alhaji asked us.

"No," I replied.

"I was supposed to come to Freetown for school, but then the war came. I heard it is a beautiful city," Alhaji said.

"Well, we'll find out soon enough. The bus is here," Mambu announced.

Soukous music was blasting inside the bus, and people were chatting loudly, as if at a marketplace. We sat in the back and watched the houses and kiosks go by. A man standing in the aisle began to dance to the music. Then a few passengers, including Mambu, joined in. We laughed and clapped for the dancers.

We got off the bus on Kissy Street, a busy area near the heart of the city. People were hurriedly going about their daily lives as if nothing were happening in the country. There were big shops on both sides of the street, and vendors crowded the tiny sidewalks. Our eyes feasted on everything, and we were quickly overwhelmed.

"I told you it would be great." Mambu jumped up in the air.

"Look at that tall building." I pointed at one.

"And that one is so tall," Alhaji called out.

"How do people get up there?" Mambu asked.

We walked slowly, admiring the number of cars, the Lebanese shops filled with all kinds of foods. My neck was hurting just from looking at the tall buildings. There were mini-markets everywhere, selling clothes, food, cassettes, stereos, and many other things. The city was too noisy, as if people were having arguments everywhere simultaneously. We wandered about all the way to the Cotton Tree, the national symbol of Sierra Leone and the landmark of the capital. We stared openmouthed at the huge tree that we had seen only on the back of currency. We now stood under it at the intersection of Siaka Stevens Street and Pademba Road, the center of the city. Its leaves were green, but the bark looked very old. "No one will believe us when we tell them this," Alhaji said as we walked away.

We walked around all day, buying ice cream and Vimto drinks. The ice cream was difficult to enjoy, as it melted too quickly under the hot sun. I spent most of my time licking the sticky residue on my elbows and between my fingers instead of eating it from the cone. As we walked around the city center, the numbers of people and cars increased. We knew no one and everyone seemed to be in a hurry. Mambu and Alhaji walked behind me the whole time and consulted with me about which way to proceed, when to stop . . . It seemed as if we were still in the front line and I was their squad leader.

It was almost evening and we had to return to the center in time for dinner. As we walked back to catch the bus, we realized that we didn't have money to pay the fare. "We should sit in front and when we get to our stop, we can jump off and run away," Mambu told us. We quietly sat on the bus, eyeing the apprentice (the conductor) who collected the fare before every stop. When the bus was about to reach our destination, the apprentice asked those getting off to raise their hands. He walked down the aisle collecting money. Then the bus stopped and the apprentice stood at the doorway, to make sure that no one got out without paying. I walked toward him, my hand in my pocket, as if I was pulling out the cash. Then I shoved him to the side and we ran away laughing. He chased us for a bit and then gave up. That night we told all the boys about the tall buildings in the city, the noise, the cars, and the markets. Everyone was excited and wanted to go to the city after that. The staff had no choice but to arrange weekend trips to the city center so that we would stop going on our own. But that wasn't enough for some of us, who wanted to visit the city more than once a week.

I do not know what happened, but people stopped buying our school supplies. Even when we offered them for a cheaper price, we were unable to get buyers. Since we didn't have any other means of getting money, we could no longer go into the city center on our own, or as frequently as we wanted. Also, attending class became the requirement for the weekend trips to the city. Because of these things, we began going to class.

It was an informal school. For mathematics, we learned addition, multiplication, and long division. For English, we read passages from books, learned to spell words, and sometimes the teacher read stories out loud and we would write them in our notebooks. It was just a way of "refreshing our memories," as the teacher put it. We didn't pay attention in class. We just wanted to be present so we wouldn't miss the trips to the city. We fought each other during lessons, sometimes stabbed each other's hands with pencils. The teacher would continue on and we would eventually stop fighting. We would then start talking about the ships we had seen from the banks of Kroo Bay, the helicopter that flew by as we walked on Lightfoot Boston Street, and at the end of class the teacher would say, "It's not your fault that you cannot sit still in class. You will be able to do so in time." We would get angry and throw pencils at him as he left the hall.

Afterward, we would have lunch, then busy ourselves playing table tennis or soccer. But at night some of us would wake up from nightmares, sweating, screaming, and punching our own heads to drive out the images that continued to torment us even when we were no longer asleep. Other boys would wake up and start choking whoever was in the bed next to theirs; they would then go running into the night after they had been restrained. The staff members were always on guard to control these sporadic outbursts. Nonetheless, every morning several of us were found hiding in the grasses by the soccer field. We didn't remember how we had gotten there.

It took several months before I began to relearn how to sleep without the aid of medicine. But even when I was finally able to fall asleep, I would start awake less than an hour later. I would dream that a faceless gunman had tied me up and begun to slit my throat with the zigzag edge of his bayonet. I would feel the pain that the knife inflicted as the man sawed my neck. I'd wake up sweating and throwing punches in the air. I would run outside to the middle of the soccer field and rock back and forth, my arms wrapped around my legs. I would try desperately to think about my childhood, but I couldn't. The war memories had formed a barrier that I had to break in order to think about any moment in my life before the war.

The rainy season in Sierra Leone falls between May and October, with the heaviest rainfalls in July, August, and September. My squad had lost the base where I had trained, and during that gunfight Moriba was killed. We left him sitting against the wall, blood coming out of his mouth, and didn't think much about him after that. Mourning the dead wasn't part of the business of killing and trying to stay alive. After that, we wandered in the forest searching for a new base before the wet season started. But we couldn't find one early enough. Most of the villages we came upon weren't suitable, since we had burned them or another group of fighters had destroyed them at some point. The lieutenant was very upset that we hadn't found a base, so he announced that we would keep walking until we found one.

At first it began to rain on and off. Then it started to rain continuously. We walked into the thickest forest and tried to escape the downpour by standing under big trees, but it rained to the point where the leaves couldn't hold off the water anymore. We walked through damp forests for weeks.

It was raining too hard one morning, and all of a sudden we were under fire. The RPGs we had failed to explode when they were fired. As a result, we retreated. The attackers didn't follow us far enough, so we regrouped again and the lieutenant said we had to counterattack immediately so that we could follow the attackers. "They will lead us to their base," he said, and we advanced toward them. We fought all day in the rain. The forest was wet and the rain washed the blood off the leaves as if cleansing the surface of the forest, but the dead bodies remained under the bushes and the blood that poured out of the bodies stayed on top of the soaked soil, as if the soil had refused to absorb any more blood for that day.

At about nightfall, the attackers began to retreat. As they were running back, they left one of their wounded men behind. We came upon him, and the lieutenant asked him where their base was. He didn't answer, so someone dragged him, with a rope around his neck, as we chased the attackers. He didn't survive the drag. At night the attackers stopped retreating. They had come to the outskirts of their base and were fighting fiercely, because they didn't want to give it up. "Hit-and-run *kalo kalo* tactics," the lieutenant ordered. We made two groups and launched the attack. The first group opened fire and pretended to retreat. The attackers chased after them, running past the ambush formed by the second group. We quietly got up and ran after the rebels, shooting them from behind. We repeated these tactics throughout the night and severely weakened the rebels. In the morning we entered the village and killed the remaining fighters, who didn't want to leave. We captured eight of their men, tied their hands and legs, and left them in the rain.

There were fireplaces in the village and lots of wood and food. The rebels had stocked up for the rainy season, but now we were the beneficiaries of the looted food and provisions. We changed into the dry clothes we could find and sat around the fire, warming ourselves and drying our shoes. I clutched my gun and smiled for a second, happy that we had found shelter. I extended my toes toward the fire to warm them and saw that they were pale and had begun to rot.

We had been in the village for only a few minutes when the rebels attacked again. They didn't want to give up the village easily. We looked

at each other sitting around the fire and angrily changed our magazines and went out to get rid of the attackers for good. We fought them
throughout the night and the following day. None of us wanted to give
up the village to the other, but in the end we killed most of the rebels
and captured a few more. The others ran away into the cold and rainy
forest. We were so angry with the prisoners that we didn't shoot them
but, rather, decided to punish them severely. "It will be a waste of bullets to shoot them," the lieutenant said. So we gave them shovels and
demanded, at gunpoint, that they dig their own graves. We sat under
the huts smoking marijuana and watched them dig in the rain. Each
time they slowed down, we would shoot around them and they would
resume digging faster. When they were done digging, we tied them and
stabbed their legs with bayonets. Some of them screamed, and we
laughed and kicked them to shut them up. We then rolled each man into
his hole and covered him with the wet mud. All of them were frightened, and they tried to get up and out of the hole as we pushed the dirt
back on them, but when they saw the tips of our guns pointed into the
hole, they lay back and watched us with their pale sad eyes. They fought
under the soil with all their might. I heard them groan underneath as
they fought for air. Gradually, they gave up, and we walked away. "At
least they are buried," one of the soldiers said, and we laughed. I
smiled a bit again as we walked back to the fire to warm ourselves.

By the fire, I realized that I had bruises on my arms, back, and foot.
Alhaji helped me attend to them with some bandages and medical supplies that the rebels had left behind. It turned out that the bruises were
from bullets that had merely torn my flesh as they missed killing me. I
was too drugged and traumatized to realize the danger of what had just
happened. I laughed as Alhaji pointed out the number of bruises on my
body.

In the morning I would feel one of the staff members wrap a blanket
around me saying, "This isn't your fault, you know. It really isn't. You'll
get through this." He would then pull me up and walk me back to
the hall.

17

I HAD NOT BEEN to the hospital since I had walked out a few months earlier, while the nurse was chatting with the sissy city lieutenant, and she had given up trying to get me to come back for a checkup. But one afternoon, during a table tennis match at which the entire staff was present, I felt someone tap me on the shoulder. It was the nurse. She was wearing a white uniform and a white hat. It was the first time I had looked at her directly. Her white teeth contrasted with her dark, shiny skin, and when she smiled, her face not only increased in beauty, it also glowed with charm. She was tall and had big brown eyes that were kind and inviting. She handed me a bottle of Coca-Cola. "Come and see me whenever you feel like it," she said, smiling, as she walked away. The Coca-Cola bottle was cold and it shocked me. I left the game hall with Alhaji and we went outside and sat on a rock drinking the soft drink. "She likes you," Alhaji teased me. I didn't say anything.

"Well, do you like her?" he asked.

"I don't know. She is older and she is our nurse," I said.

"You mean you are afraid of women," Alhaji replied, nodding.

"I don't think she likes me the way you are thinking about it." I looked at Alhaji, who was laughing at what I had said.

After we finished the bottle, Alhaji left and I decided to go to the hospital. When I got to the entrance, I peeked in and saw the nurse on the phone. She motioned for me to come inside and sit. She smiled and made sure that I noticed that it was because of my presence and not her phone conversation. I looked around and saw a chart on the wall with all the names of the boys at the center. In the boxes beside most of the names there was a check indicating that they had been to at least one session. There was nothing in the boxes across from my name. The nurse took the chart down and put it into a drawer as she hung up the phone. She pulled her chair closer to me and I thought she was going to ask me a question about the war, but instead she calmly asked, "What is your name?" I was surprised, since I was certain that she knew my name. "You know my name," I angrily said.

"Maybe I do, but I want you to tell me your name," she insisted, widening her eyes.

"Okay, okay. Ishmael," I said.

"Great name." She nodded and continued. "My name is Esther and we should be friends."

"Are you sure you want to be friends with me?" I asked. She thought for a while and said, "Maybe not."

I was quiet for a bit, as I didn't know what to say and also didn't trust anyone at this point in my life. I had learned to survive and take care of myself. I had done just that for most of my short life, with no one to trust, and frankly, I liked being alone, since it made surviving easier. People like the lieutenant, whom I had obeyed and trusted, had made me question trusting anyone, especially adults. I was very suspicious of people's intentions. I had come to believe that people befriended only to exploit one another. So I ignored the nurse and began to stare out the window.

"I am your nurse and that's all. If you want to be friends with me, you will have to ask me and I will have to trust you first," she said. I smiled, because I was thinking the same thing. She was perplexed at first by the sudden smile. But then she said, "You have a great smile, you should smile more." I stopped immediately and tensed my face.

"Is there anything that you want from the city?" she asked, but I didn't answer.

"That's it for today," she said.

A few days after that first conversation, the nurse gave me a present. I was watching some of the boys roll a volleyball net onto the yard. Alhaji returned from his session at the hospital and told me that nurse Esther said I should go see her. I wanted to watch the volleyball game, but Alhaji began to pull me and didn't let go until we were at the doorway of the hospital. He then shoved me inside and ran away giggling. Lying on the floor, I looked up to see Esther sitting behind her desk, smiling.

"Alhaji said you want to see me," I said, getting to my feet.

She threw a package at me. I held it in my hand, wondering what it was and why she had gotten it for me. She was looking at me, waiting for me to open it. When I unwrapped it, I jumped up and hugged her, but immediately held back my happiness. I sternly asked, "Why did you get me this Walkman and cassette if we are not friends? And how did you know that I like rap music?"

"Please sit down," she said, taking the package from me, putting the battery and cassette in the Walkman, and handing it to me. I put the headphones on and there was Run-D.M.C.: "*It's like that, and that the way it is . . .*" coming through the headphones. I began to shake my head, then Esther lifted the headphones off my ears and said, "I have to examine you while you listen to the music." I agreed, and took off my shirt, stood on a scale, and she checked my tongue, used a flashlight to look into my eyes . . . I didn't care because the song had taken hold of me, and I listened closely to every word. But when she began examining my legs and saw the scars on my left shin, she took my headphones off again and asked, "How did you get these scars?"

"Bullet wounds," I casually replied.

Her face filled with sorrow and her voice was shaking when she spoke: "You have to tell me what happened so I can prescribe treatment." At first I was reluctant, but she said she would be able to treat

me effectively only if I told her what had happened, especially about
how my bullet wounds were treated. So I told her the whole story
about how I got shot, not because I really wanted to, but because I
thought that if I told her some of the gruesome truth of my war years
she would be afraid of me and would cease asking questions. She listened attentively when I began to talk. Her eyes were glued to my face,
and I bowed my head as I delved into my recent past.

During the second dry season of my war years, we were low on food
and ammunition. So, as usual, we decided to attack another village.
First, I went with my squad to spy on a village. We watched the village
all day and saw that there were more men than us and that they were
well armed and had newer guns. I am not sure if they were rebels,
because they had fewer boys than any of the other groups we had
attacked. Half wore army uniforms and half civilian clothes. We returned to base and I reported my squad's findings to the lieutenant.
We immediately left for the village, which was about three days' walk.
The plan was to first secure the village, then remain there and form a
new base instead of bringing the goods back.

We left our village that night, alternately walking fast and jogging
on the path all night. During the three-day journey, we stopped once
a day to eat, drink, and take drugs. We carried with us all the ammunition, guns, and semiautomatic machine guns. Each of us had two
guns, one strapped to our back, the other held in our hands. We left
only two men behind to guard the base. On the morning of the third
day, the lieutenant made us rest longer than we had during the previous days. Afterward, we walked all day and into the evening until the
village was in sight.

There were many mango, orange, and guava trees in the village,
and it looked as if it had been a farm. Surrounding it, we waited for the
lieutenant's command. As we lay in ambush, we began to realize that
the place was empty. I was lying next to the lieutenant and he looked
at me with a puzzled face. I whispered to him that the village had been
full of gunmen a few days ago, even though it now looked deserted. As

we continued to watch, a dog strolled across the village, barking as it went down the path. About an hour later, five gunmen entered the village. They took buckets from the verandah of one of the houses and headed toward the river. We were beginning to suspect that something was amiss when a shot was fired from behind us. It was clear now: we were being ambushed. The attackers wanted to push us toward the village so they could have us in the open.

We exchanged fire all night, until morning arrived, at which point we had no choice but to retreat into the village where they wanted us. We had already lost about five men, and the rebels were coming at the rest of us. They were up in the mango, orange, and guava trees, ready to rain bullets down on us. My squad scattered, running from one end of the village to the other, crouching behind houses. We had to get out before it was too late, but first we had to get rid of the attackers in the trees, which we did by spraying bullets into the branches to make the rebels fall off them. Those who didn't immediately die we shot before they landed on the ground. To avoid the open area and regroup in the nearby forest, we had to make an opening for ourselves; there was too much firepower surrounding us. So we concentrated our firepower on one area of the forest until everyone was dead. As soon as we had time to gather, the lieutenant once again gave us his little talk about how we had to fight fiercely to capture the village, otherwise we would have to roam the forest looking for another base.

Some people were injured, but not so severely as to keep them from fighting; others, like myself, had received many bullet wounds that they ignored. Our first counterattack was carried out in order to secure ammunition from the dead. Then we launched a second fierce attack to gain some control of the village. For more than twenty-four hours we retreated and attacked, using the arms and ammunition from those we had killed. Finally it seemed we had overpowered our rivals. The gunshots had stopped. The bushes behind the mango trees were still. The village, it seemed, was ours.

I was filling my backpack with ammunition from a hut when bullets began to rain on the village again. I was hit three times on my left foot. The first two bullets went in and out, and the last one stayed inside my foot. I couldn't walk, so I lay on the ground and shot into the bush where the bullets that hit me had come from. I released the entire round of the magazine into that one area. I remember feeling a tingle in my spine, but I was too drugged to really feel the pain, even though my foot had begun to swell. The sergeant doctor in my squad dragged me into one of the houses and tried to remove the bullet. Each time he raised his hands from my wound, I saw my blood all over his fingers. He constantly wiped my forehead with a soaked cloth. My eyes began to grow heavy and I fainted.

I do not know what happened, but when I woke up the next day I felt as if I had had nails hammered into the bones of my foot and my veins were being chiseled. I felt so much pain that I was unable to cry out loud; tears just fell from my eyes. The ceiling of the thatched-roof house where I was lying on a bed was blurry. My eyes struggled to become familiar with my surroundings. The gunfire had ceased and the village was quiet, so I assumed that the attackers had been successfully driven away. I felt a brief relief for that, but the pain in my foot returned, causing the veins in my entire body to tighten. I tucked my lips in, closed my heavy eyelids, and held tight to the edges of the wooden bed. I heard footsteps of people entering the house. They stood by my bed, and as soon as they began to speak, I recognized their voices.

"The boy is suffering and we have no medicine here to lessen his pain. Everything is at our former base." The sergeant doctor sighed and continued. "It will take six days to send someone to get the medicine and return. He will die from the pain by then."

"We have to send him to the former base, then. We need those provisions from that base, anyway. Do all you can to make sure that the boy stays alive," the lieutenant said, and walked out.

"Yes, sir," the sergeant doctor said, and sighed even longer. I slowly opened my eyes, and this time I could see clearly. I looked at his sweaty face and tried to smile a little. After having heard what they said, I swore to myself that I would fight hard and do anything for my squad after my foot was healed.

"We will get you some help. Just be strong, young man," the sergeant doctor said gently, sitting by my bed and examining my leg.

"Yes, sir," I said, and tried to raise my hand to salute him, but he tenderly brought my hand down.

Two soldiers came into the house and told the sergeant doctor that the lieutenant had sent them to help take me back to our former base. They took me off the bed, placed me in a hammock, and carried me outside. The sun blinded me at first, and then the treetops of the village began to spin around as they carried me out of the village. The journey felt as if it took a month. I fainted and awoke many times, and each time I opened my eyes, it seemed as if the voices of those who carried me were fading into the distance.

Finally, we got to the base and the sergeant doctor went to work on me. I was injected with something. I had no idea we had needles at the base, but in my condition I couldn't ask what was happening. I was given cocaine, as I frantically demanded it. The doctor started operating on me before the drugs took effect. The other soldiers held my hands and stuffed a cloth into my mouth. The doctor stuck a crooked-looking scissors inside my wound and fished for the bullet. I could feel the edge of the metal inside me. My entire body was racked with pain. My bones became sour. Just when I thought I had had enough, the doctor abruptly pulled the bullet out. A piercing pain rushed up my spine from my waist to the back of my neck. I fainted.

When I regained consciousness, it was the morning of the next day and the drugs had kicked in. I looked about the room and saw on the table the instruments that had been used for my operation. Next to the instruments was a piece of cloth soaked with blood and I wondered how much blood I had lost during the operation. I reached my hands down to my foot and felt the bandage before I stood up and limped outside, where some soldiers and the sergeant were sitting. "Where is my weapon?" I asked them. The sergeant handed me the G3 that was on top of the mortar, and I began cleaning it. I shot a couple of rounds sitting against a wall, ignoring the bandage on my foot and everyone else. I smoked marijuana, ate, and snorted cocaine and *brown brown*. That was all I did for three days before we left for the new base we had captured. When we left, we threw kerosene on the thatched-roof houses, lit them with matches, and fired a couple of RPGs into the walls. We always destroyed the bases we abandoned so that other squads wouldn't be able to use them. Two soldiers carried me in the hammock, but this time I had my gun and I looked left and right as we traveled the forest path.

At the new base, I stayed put for three weeks and appointed Alhaji to be in charge of my expedition squad. I busied myself with drugs and cleaning my gun. The sergeant doctor cleaned my wounds and would always say, "You are lucky." At that time I didn't think I was lucky, I thought I was brave and knew how to fight. Little did I know that surviving the war that I was in, or any other kind of war, was not a matter of feeling trained or brave. These were just things that made me feel I was immune from death.

At the end of the three weeks, we had the first batch of attackers; the lieutenant knew they were coming. I tightened the bandage around my foot, picked up my gun, and followed my squad to ambush the attackers before they got anywhere near our village. We killed most of them and captured a few whom we brought back to base. "These are the men responsible for the bullet holes in your foot. It's time to make sure they never shoot at you or your comrades." The lieutenant pointed at the prisoners. I am not sure if one of the captives was the shooter, but any captive would do at that time. So they were all lined up, six of them, with their hands tied. I shot them on their feet and watched them suffer for an entire day before finally shooting them in the head so that they would stop crying. Before I shot each man, I looked at him and saw how his eyes gave up hope and steadied before I pulled the trigger. I found their somber eyes irritating.

When I finished telling Esther the story, she had tears in her eyes and she couldn't decide whether to rub my head or hug me. In the end she

but said, "None of what happened was your fault. You
little boy, and anytime you want to tell me anything, I am
listen." She stared at me, trying to catch my eye so she could
assure me of what she had just said. I became angry and regretted that
I had told someone, a civilian, about my experience. I hated the "It is
not your fault" line that all the staff members said every time anyone
spoke about the war.

I got up, and as I started walking out of the hospital, Esther began
to speak. "I will arrange for a full checkup at the Connaught hospital."
She paused and then continued, "Let me keep the Walkman. You don't
want the others to envy you and steal it. I will be here every day, so you
can come and listen to it anytime." I threw the Walkman at her and
left, putting my fingers in my ears so I couldn't hear her say "It is not
your fault."

That night, as I sat on the verandah listening to some of the boys discuss the volleyball game I had missed, I tried to think about my childhood days, but it was impossible, as I began getting flashbacks of the
first time I slit a man's throat. The scene kept surfacing in my memory
like lightning on a dark rainy night, and each time it happened, I
heard a sharp cry in my head that made my spine hurt. I went inside
and sat on my bed facing the wall and tried to stop thinking, but I had
a severe migraine that night. I rolled my head on the cold cement floor,
but it didn't stop. I went to the shower room and put my head under
the cold water, but that didn't help either. The headache became so severe that I couldn't walk. I began to cry out loud. The night nurse was
called. She gave me some sleeping tablets, but I still couldn't fall asleep,
even after my migraine stopped. I couldn't face the nightmares I knew
would come.

Esther got me to tell her some of my dreams. She would just listen and
sit quietly with me. If she wanted to say anything, she would first ask,
"Would you like me to say something about your dream?" Mostly I
would say no and ask for the Walkman.

One afternoon Esther wasn't supposed to work, but she came to the center wearing a jeans skirt instead of her normal white uniform. She came in a white Toyota with two men. One of the men was the driver and the other was a field-worker for Children Associated with the War (CAW). This was a Catholic organization that partnered with UNICEF and NGOs to create centers like ours.

"We are going to the hospital for your examination, and after that we will give you a tour of the city." Esther was excited. "What do you say?" she asked me.

"Okay," I agreed. I was always excited to go to the city. "Can my friend Alhaji come?" I asked.

"Sure," she said, as if she knew I would ask.

As we drove into Freetown, the field-worker introduced himself: "My name is Leslie, it is a pleasure to meet you gentlemen." He turned around from the front seat and shook our hands. He sat back and studied us in the rearview mirror. Esther sat between Alhaji and me in the backseat. She tickled us and sometimes put her arms around us. I resisted this affection, and she would put both her arms around Alhaji. I would look away and she would softly elbow me before putting her arms around me again.

At the center of the city, Esther pointed out the post office, shops, the UN building, and the Cotton Tree. On Wallace Johnson Street, traders played loud music and rang bells to attract customers. Boys and girls carried coolers on their heads, shouting, "Cold ice, cold ice . . ." "Cold ginger beer . . ." The city always amazed me, with its busy people hurrying up and down and its traders noisily creating its unique sound. I was watching one ringing a bell and throwing the secondhand clothes he was selling up in the air to attract passersby, when our car stopped at the hospital where I was to be examined.

The doctor kept asking, "You feel anything?" as he touched and squeezed parts of my body where I had been wounded or shot. I was beginning to get upset, when he told me he was finished. I put my clothes on and came into the waiting area where Esther, Leslie, and Alhaji sat. They were smiling, and Esther walked up and pulled on my nose to cheer me up. We strolled over to the market area we had driven past. I spent most of my time studying a rack of cassettes under a kiosk. Esther and Alhaji looked at soccer jerseys, and she bought him one. Leslie bought me a Bob Marley cassette. It was the *Exodus* album. I grew up on reggae music but had not heard it for a while. As I looked at the cassette, trying to remember the songs, my head began to hurt. Esther must have noticed what was happening to me, because she took the cassette from me and put it in her bag. "Who wants Coca-Cola?" she asked. I was excited and ran ahead to the Coca-Cola stand. She bought us each a bottle. It was cold and it teased my teeth. I savored it as we drove back to the center. I was in high spirits, smiling all the way.

Leslie took this opportunity to tell me that he had been assigned to me and a few other boys. Part of his job was to find a place for me to live after I had completed my rehabilitation. "If you ever need to talk to me at any time, go to Esther's office and she will call me, okay?" I nodded in agreement, with the Coca-Cola bottle in my mouth.

Before Esther got into the car that evening to go home, she pulled me aside and crouched down to look at me directly. I avoided eye contact, but she wasn't discouraged. She said, "I will keep the Bob Marley tape and bring it back tomorrow. So come by and listen to it."

She got in the car and waved as they drove off. Alhaji had already put on his jersey and was running around playing imaginary soccer. When we got back to the verandah, everyone marveled at Alhaji's new jersey. It was green, white, and blue, the colors of the national flag, and it had number 11 on the back. Alhaji walked up and down the verandah showing off. He finally stopped and announced, "I know the city like the back of my hand. I know where to get the goods."

He wore the jersey for almost a week without taking it off except to shower, because he knew that someone would try to steal it. He began doing business with his shirt. He would lend it to the boys for a few hours in exchange for toothpaste, soap, lunch, and so on. At the end of the week, he had a lot of toothpaste and other items that he sold at an outdoor market farther away from the center.

The day after we returned from the city, I went to the hospital immediately after class and waited for Esther. She was surprised to find me waiting for her at the doorstep. She rubbed my head and said, "I have good news. Your results from the test came. The doctor said nothing is seriously wrong. I just have to make sure you take certain medicines and in a few months we will do another checkup." She opened the door and I followed her without saying a word. She knew what I wanted. She gave me the Bob Marley cassette and the Walkman, along with a really nice notebook and pen.

"You can write the lyrics of the songs you like on the album and we can learn to sing them together, if you want." She began making a call.

How did she know I loved to write song lyrics? I thought, but didn't ask. Later, after I had been rehabilitated, I learned that Esther knew what I was interested in through the informal schooling at the center. In the short classes that we attended, we had been given questionnaires as a form of exam. The questions were general in the beginning. They didn't provoke any difficult memories. What kind of music do you like? Do you like reggae music? If so, who do you like? What do you listen to music for? These were the sorts of questions we would either discuss in class or write a short answer to. Our answers were then given to the nurses or whoever was in charge of our individual counseling sessions.

I began to look forward to Esther's arrival in the afternoons. I sang for her the parts of songs I had memorized that day. Memorizing lyrics left me little time to think about what had happened in the war. As I grew comfortable with Esther, I talked to her mainly about Bob Marley's lyrics and Run-D.M.C.'s, too. She mostly listened. Twice a week Leslie came and went over the lyrics with me. He loved telling me the history of Rastafarianism. I loved the history of Ethiopia and the story of the meeting of the Queen of Sheba and King Solomon. I related to the long distance they traveled and their determination to reach their chosen destination. I wished that my journey had been as meaningful and as full of merriment as theirs.

It happened one night after I had fallen asleep while reading the lyrics of a song. I had not slept well for months now, and so far I had been able to avoid my nightmares by busying myself day and night with listening to and writing the lyrics of Bob Marley's songs. But that night I had a nightmare that was different from the ones I had been having. It began with my swimming in a river at Mattru Jong with my brother Junior. We dove to the bottom of the river and brought out oysters. We placed them on a rock and plunged to the deep again. We were competing with each other. In the end Junior got more oysters than I did. We ran home for dinner, racing each other. When we got there, the food was sitting in pots, but no one was around. I turned to ask my brother what was happening, but he was gone. I was alone and it was dark. I searched for a lamp and found it, but I was afraid. My forehead was sweating. I took the lamp to the living room, where a box of matches sat on the table. I lit the lamp, and as soon as the room was bright, I saw men standing all around. They had circled me in the dark. I could see their bodies—except for their faces, which were darker, as if they were headless walking beings. Some were barefoot and others wore army boots. All had guns and knives. They began to shoot, stab, and slice each other's throats. But they would rise and then get killed again. Their blood began to fill the room, its tide quickly rising. They wailed, causing me great anguish. I held my ears to stop hearing them, but I began to feel their pain. Each time a person was stabbed, I felt it worse; I saw the blood dripping from the same part of my body as that of the victim. I began to cry as the blood filled the room. The men disappeared and the door immediately opened, letting the blood out with a rush. I went outside with the blood all over me and saw my mother, father, older and younger brother. They were all smiling as if nothing had happened, as if we had been together all this time.

"Sit down, Mr. Troublesome," my father said.

"Don't mind him," my mother chuckled.

I sat down facing my father, but couldn't eat with them. My body had gotten numb, and my family didn't seem to notice that I was covered with blood. It began to rain and my family ran into the house, leaving me outside. I sat in the rain for a while, letting it clean the blood off me. I got up to go into the house, but it wasn't there. It had disappeared.

I was looking around confused when I woke up from the dream.

I had fallen off my bed.

I got up and went outside and sat on the stoop looking into the night. I was still confused, as I couldn't tell whether I had had a dream or not. It was the first time I had dreamt of my family since I started running away from the war.

The next afternoon I went to see Esther, and she could tell that something was bothering me. "Do you want to lie down?" she asked, almost whispering.

"I had this dream last night. I don't know what to make of it," I said, looking away.

She came and sat next to me and asked, "Would you like to tell me about it?"

I didn't reply.

"Or just talk about it out loud and pretend I am not here. I won't say anything. Only if you ask me." She sat quietly beside me. The quietness lasted for a while, and for some reason I began to tell her my dream.

At first she just listened to me, and then gradually she started asking questions to make me talk about the lives I had lived before and during the war. "None of these things are your fault," she would always say sternly at the end of every conversation. Even though I had heard that phrase from every staff member—and frankly I had always hated it—I began that day to believe it. It was the genuine tone in Esther's voice that made the phrase finally begin to sink into my mind and heart. That didn't make me immune from the guilt that I felt for what I had done. Nonetheless, it lightened my burdensome

memories and gave me strength to think about things. The more I
spoke about my experiences to Esther, the more I began to cringe at
the gruesome details, even though I didn't let her know that. I didn't
completely trust Esther. I only liked talking to her because I felt that
she didn't judge me for what I had been a part of; she looked at me
with the same inviting eyes and welcoming smile that said I was a child.

One evening Esther took me to her house and made me dinner. After dinner we went for a walk in the city. We went to the wharf at the
end of Rawdon Street. The moon was out that night and we sat at
the jetty and watched it. I told Esther about the shapes I used to see in
the moon when I was much younger. She was fascinated. We looked
at the moon and described the shapes we saw to each other. I saw the
woman cradling the baby in her arms, just as I used to. On our way
back to her house, I didn't look at the city lights any longer. I looked
into the sky and felt as if the moon was following us.

When I was a child, my grandmother told me that the sky speaks
to those who look and listen to it. She said, "In the sky there are
always answers and explanations for everything: every pain, every
suffering, joy, and confusion." That night I wanted the sky to talk
to me.

18

ONE DAY DURING MY FIFTH MONTH at Benin Home, I was sitting on a rock behind the classrooms when Esther came by. She sat next to me without uttering a word. She had my lyrics notebook in her hand. "I feel as if there is nothing left for me to be alive for," I said slowly. "I have no family, it is just me. No one will be able to tell stories about my childhood." I sniffled a bit.

Esther put her arms around me and pulled me closer to her. She shook me to get my full attention before she started. "Think of me as your family, your sister."

"But I didn't have a sister," I replied.

"Well, now you do. You see, this is the beauty of starting a new family. You can have different kinds of family members." She looked at me directly, waiting for me to say something.

"Okay, you can be my sister—temporarily." I emphasized the last word.

"That is fine with me. So will you come to see your temporary sister tomorrow, please." She covered her face as if she would be sad if I said no.

"Okay, okay, no need to be sad," I said, and we both laughed a bit.

Esther's laugh always reminded me of Abigail, a girl I had seen during my first two semesters of secondary school in Bo Town. Sometimes I wished Esther was Abigail, so that we could talk about past times before the war. I wanted us to laugh with all our beings, longer and without any worries, as I had done with Abigail but couldn't anymore. At the end of each laugh there was always some feeling of sadness that I couldn't escape.

At times I stared at Esther while she was busy doing paperwork. Whenever she sensed my eyes examining her face, she would throw a folded paper at me without looking in my direction. I would smile and put the folded paper in my pocket, pretending that the blank paper was a special note she had written to me.

That afternoon, as Esther walked away from where I sat on the rock, she continually turned around to wave at me, until she disappeared behind one of the halls. I smiled back and forgot about my loneliness for the time being.

The following day Esther told me that there were visitors coming to the center. The staff had asked the boys to hold a talent show. Basically, we were all supposed to do anything that we were good at.

"You can sing your reggae songs," Esther suggested.

"How about a Shakespeare monologue?" I asked.

"Okay, but I still think you should do some music." She put her arms around me. I had become very fond of Esther, but refused to show it. Whenever she hugged me or put her arms around me, I would quickly break loose. Whenever she left, though, I watched her go. She had a unique and graceful walk. It was almost as if she sailed on the ground. I would always run to see her after class to tell her about my day. My friends Mambu and Alhaji made fun of me. "Your girlfriend is here, Ishmael. Are we going to see you at all this afternoon?"

The visitors from the European Commission, the UN, UNICEF, and several NGOs arrived at the center in a convoy of cars one afternoon. They wore suits and ties and shook hands with each other before they started walking around the center. Some of the boys followed behind them, and I sat on the verandah with Mambu. All of the visitors were smiling, sometimes adjusting their ties or taking notes on the writing pads they carried. Some of them looked into our sleeping places, and the others took off their jackets and played hand-wrestling games and tug-of-war with boys. Afterward, they were shepherded into the dining room, which had been set up quite nicely for the talent show. Mr. Kamara, the director of the center, gave a few remarks, and then boys started telling Bra Spider and monster stories and performing tribal dances. I read a monologue from *Julius Caesar* and performed a short hip-hop play about the redemption of a former child soldier that I had written with Esther's encouragement.

After that event, I became popular at the center. Mr. Kamara called me to his office one morning and said, "You and your friends really impressed those visitors. They know now that it is possible for you boys to be rehabilitated." I was just happy to have had the chance to perform again, in peace. But Mr. Kamara was in high spirits.

"How would you like to be the spokesperson for this center?" he asked me.

"Ah! What will I have to do or say?" I hesitantly asked. I was beginning to think that this whole thing was being blown out of proportion.

"Well, to begin with, if there is an event on the issue of child soldiers, we will write you something to read. Once you get comfortable, you can begin writing your own speech, or whatever you want." Mr. Kamara's serious face told me he meant what he was saying. Not more than a week later, I was talking at gatherings in Freetown about child soldiering and how it must be stopped. "We can be rehabilitated," I would emphasize, and point to myself as an example. I would always tell people that I believe children have the resilience to outlive their sufferings, if given a chance.

I was at the end of my sixth month when my childhood friend Mohamed arrived at the center. The last time I had seen him was when I left Mogbwemo with Talloi and Junior for a performance in Mattru Jong. He couldn't come with us that day as he was helping his father

kitchen. I had often wondered about what had hap-
, but I never thought I would see him again. I was return-
gathering at St. Edward's Secondary School that evening
this light-skinned, skinny boy with bony cheeks sitting on
the stoop by himself. He looked familiar, but I wasn't sure if I knew
him. As I approached, he jumped up.

"Hey, man, remember me?" he exclaimed, and began doing the
running man and singing "Here Comes the Hammer."

I joined him, and we did some of the moves we had learned together for a group dance to this particular song. We high-fived each
other and then hugged. He was still taller than me. We sat together on
the stoop and briefly talked about our childhood pranks. "Sometimes
I think about those great times we had dancing at talent shows, prac-
ticing new dances, playing soccer until we couldn't see the ball . . . It
seems like all those things happened a very long time ago. It is really
strange, you know," he said, looking away for a bit.

"I know, I know . . ." I said.

"You were a troublesome boy," he reminded me.

"I know, I know . . ."

It was at the beginning of my seventh month at the rehabilitation center when Leslie came again to have a chat. I was called to a room in the
hospital where he waited. When I walked into the room, he stood up
to greet me. His face showed both grief and happiness. I had to ask
him what the matter was.

"Are you all right?" I studied him.

"Yes." He scratched his head and mumbled something to himself.
"I am sorry about bringing up this matter again. I know it will upset
you, but I have to be honest with you," Leslie said. He walked around
the room and began: "We cannot locate any immediate family member of yours, so we have to find you a foster family here in the city. I
hope that will be fine with you. I will check on you after you've completed your rehabilitation to see how you are doing in your new life."

He sat down and, looking at me, continued, "Well, do you have any concerns or questions?"

"Yes, I think so," I said. I told him that before the war my father had spoken about my uncle, who lived in the city. I did not even know what he looked like, much less where he lived.

"What is his name?" Leslie asked.

"His name is Tommy and my father told me he is a carpenter," I replied.

Leslie was writing my mysterious uncle's name in his notebook. After he was done scribbling his notes, he said, "No promises, but I will see what I can find out. I will get back to you soon." He paused, tapped me on the shoulder, and continued, "I hear you are doing great. Keep it up."

He walked out of the room. I didn't count on him being able to find my uncle in such a big city, especially with the little information I had provided. I left the room and went to see Esther at the other side of the building. She was busy putting away the new supplies of bandages and medicines in the cabinets that hung on the walls of the room. As soon as she noticed that I was standing in the doorway, she began to smile, but continued doing her work. I sat and waited for her to finish.

"So how did the meeting with Leslie go?" she asked as she put the last box of medicine away. I told her everything he had said, ending with my skepticism about whether Leslie would be able to find my uncle. She listened carefully and said, "You never know. He might find him."

One Saturday afternoon, as I chatted with Esther and Mohamed, Leslie walked in, smiling widely. I suspected he had found me a foster home and that I was going to be "repatriated"—the term used to describe the process of reuniting ex–child soldiers with their former communities.

"What is the good news?" Esther asked. Leslie examined my curious face, then walked back to the door and opened it. A tall man walked in. He had a wide, genuine smile that made his face look like a little boy's. His hands were long and he looked at me directly, smiling. He wasn't as light-skinned as my father.

"This is your uncle," Leslie proudly announced.

"How de body, Ishmael?" the man said, and walked over to where I was sitting. He bent over and embraced me long and hard. My arms hung loose at my sides.

What if he is just some man pretending to be my uncle? I thought. The man let go of me. He was crying, which is when I began to believe that he was really my family, because his crying was genuine and men in my culture rarely cried.

He crouched on his heels next to me and began, "I am sorry I never came to see you all those years. I wish I had met you before today. But we can't go back now. We just have to start from here. I am sorry for your losses. Leslie told me everything." He looked at Leslie with thankful eyes and continued, "After you are done here, you can come and live with me. You are my son. I don't have much, but I will give you a place to sleep, food, and my love." He put his arms around me.

No one had called me son in a very long time. I didn't know what to say. Everyone, it seemed, was waiting for my response. I turned to my uncle, smiled at him, and said, "Thank you for coming to see me. I really appreciate that you have offered me to stay with you. But I don't even know you." I put my head down.

"Like I said, we cannot go back. But we can start from here. I am your family and that is enough for us to begin liking each other," he replied, rubbing my head and laughing a little.

I got up and hugged my uncle, and he embraced me harder than he had the first time and kissed me on my forehead. We briefly stood in silence before he began to speak again. "I can't stay long, because I have to finish some work at the other part of the city. But from now on, I will visit you every weekend. And if it is okay, I would like you to come home with me at some point, to see where I live and to meet my wife and children—your family." My uncle's voice trembled; he was trying to hold back sobs. He rubbed my head with one hand and shook Leslie's hand with the other.

"Sir, from now on, you will be informed about how this young man is doing," Leslie said.

"Thank you," my uncle replied. He held my hand and I walked with him toward the van that he and Leslie had arrived in. Before my uncle got into the car with Leslie, he hugged me again and said, "You look like your father, and you remind me of him when we were growing up. I hope you are not as stubborn as he was." He laughed, and I did, too. Esther, Mohamed, and I waved them off.

"He seems like a nice man," Esther said as soon as the van disappeared from our sight.

"Congratulations, man, you have a family member in the city away from all the madness," Mohamed said.

"I guess so," I said, but I didn't know what to do in my happy state. I was still hesitant to let myself let go, because I still believed in the fragility of happiness.

"Come on, man, cheer up." Mohamed pulled my ears, and he and Esther lifted me up and carried me back to the hospital, laughing. At the hospital Esther put the Bob Marley cassette on the tape player, and we all began to mime "Three Little Birds" together. "Don't worry about a thing," we sang, "'cause every little thing gonna be all right . . ."

That night I sat on the verandah with Mambu, Alhaji, and Mohamed. We were quiet, as usual. The sound of an ambulance somewhere in the city took over the silence of the night. I began to wonder about what my uncle was doing at that moment. I imagined him gathering his family to tell them about me. I could see him sobbing during his account and his family gradually joining him in crying. Part of me wanted them to cry as much as they could before I met them, as I always felt uncomfortable when people cried because of what I had been through. I looked at Alhaji and Mambu, who were staring into the dark night. I wanted to tell them about the discovery of my uncle, but I felt guilty, since no one from their families had been found. I also didn't want to destroy the silence that had returned after the ambulance's wailing died down.

As my uncle promised, he came to visit every weekend.

"My uncle is coming. I saw him down the road by the mango tree," I told Esther the first weekend after his initial visit.

"You sound excited." She put her pen down. She examined my face for a while and then continued. "I told you he seemed like a good man."

My uncle walked through the door and wiped his sweaty forehead with his handkerchief before hugging me. He said hello to Esther during our embrace. As soon as we stood apart, he began to smile so widely that my face relaxed and I too began to smile. He put his bag on the floor and pulled out some biscuits and a bottle of cold ginger beer.

"I thought you might need some fuel for our walk," he said as he handed me the presents.

"You two should take the gravel road up the hill," Esther suggested. My uncle and I nodded in agreement.

"I won't be here when you return. It is nice meeting you again, sir," she said, looking at my uncle. She turned toward me. "I will see you tomorrow."

My uncle and I left the hospital room and started walking in the direction Esther had suggested. We were quiet at first. I listened to the sound of our footsteps on the dusty road. I could hear the rattling of lizards crossing the road to climb the nearby mango tree. I could feel my uncle's eyes on me.

"How is everything? Are they treating you well at this place?" my uncle asked.

"Everything is fine here," I replied.

"I hope you are not as quiet as your father." He wiped his forehead again and then asked, "Did your father ever talk about his home?"

"Sometimes he did, although not as much as I wished he had." I raised my lowered head and briefly met my uncle's kind, inviting eyes before looking away. The gravel road was getting narrower as we approached the bottom of the hill. I told him that my father had mentioned him in every one of his stories of a troublesome childhood. Told him that my father had recounted to me about the time they went to the bush to fetch firewood and accidentally shook a beehive. The bees chased them and they ran toward the village. Since my father was shorter, most of the bees concentrated on my uncle's head. They ran and dove into a river, but the bees circled on top of the water waiting for them to resurface. They had to catch their breath, so they got out of the water and ran to their village, bringing the bees with them.

"Yes, I remember. Everyone was upset with us for bringing the bees to the village, because they stung the old men who couldn't run fast and some younger children. Your father and I locked the door, hid under the bed, and laughed at the commotion." My uncle was giggling and I couldn't help but laugh. After he stopped laughing, he sighed and said, "Ah, your father and I, we did too many troublesome things. If you are as troublesome as we were, I will give you some leeway, because it wouldn't be fair for me to get down on you." He put his arm around my shoulder.

"I think my troublesome days are long gone," I said sadly.

"Ah, you are still a boy, you have time to be a little more troublesome," my uncle said. We became quiet again and listened to the evening wind whizzing through the trees.

I loved the walks with my uncle, because they gave me a chance to talk about my childhood, about growing up with my father and older brother. I needed to talk about those good times before the war. But the more I talked about my father, the more I missed my mother and little brother, too. I didn't grow up with them. I felt as if I missed that chance and would never get it again, and that made me sad. I spoke to my uncle about it, but he just listened, because he knew neither my mother nor my little brother. So in order to balance things out for me, he made me talk about the time my family lived in Mattru Jong, when my parents were together. Even then, there wasn't that much to say, as my parents separated when I was very young.

I got to know my uncle quite well during our walks, and I began to eagerly await his arrival on weekends. He always brought me a present and would tell me about his week. He talked about the roof he had built for someone's house, the beautiful table he had to complete the next day by polishing it, how well my cousins were doing in school. He said hello from his wife. I in turn would tell him about the table tennis and soccer tournaments I had participated in, the performance we had given for visitors, if there was any that week. We walked so many times on the same gravel road that I could close my eyes and still avoid all the big rocks on the road.

One weekend my uncle took me to meet his family. It was a Saturday and the sun was so bright that we couldn't see our shadows on the ground. He lived in New England Ville, a hilly area in the western part of Freetown. My uncle came to Benin Home earlier than usual to get me. We took a noisy lorry to the center of the city. My uncle and I were quiet for a while, but began to laugh, because the two men sitting next to us were discussing which palm wine was better, one that was tapped from a standing palm tree or one from a fallen tree. The men were still arguing when we got off the lorry. We walked slowly toward my uncle's house, his arm around my shoulders. I was happy walking with my uncle, but I worried whether his family would accept me the way he had—without asking me anything about my war years.

As we walked up the hill, nearing my uncle's home, he pulled me aside and said, "I told only my wife about your past life as a soldier. I kept it secret from my children. I don't think they will understand now as my wife and I do. I hope it is okay with you." Relieved, I nodded, and we continued on.

Immediately after a bend and a rise on the gravel road we came upon my uncle's house. It overlooked the city, and from the verandah one could see the ships in the bay. It was a beautiful view of the city, this place that was to become my home. The house had no electricity or running water, and the kitchen that stood apart from the house was made entirely of zinc. Under a mango tree a few meters from the yard was the latrine and the *kule*—open-air shower. It reminded me of Mattru Jong.

When we walked onto the verandah, my uncle's wife came out, her face glowing as if she had polished it all her life. She stood at the doorway and tied her wrapper before proceeding to embrace me so tightly that I felt my nose and lips being squashed against her arms. She released me, stood back, and pinched my cheeks.

"Welcome, my son," she said. She was a short woman with very dark skin, round cheekbones, and bright eyes. My uncle didn't have children of his own, so he raised the children of family members as his own. There were four of them—Allie, the oldest one; Matilda; Kona; and Sombo, the littlest, who was six years old. They had all stopped doing their chores and came onto the verandah to hug their "brother," as my uncle explained my relation to them.

"It is good to have another boy in the family," Allie said after he hugged me. He and my uncle laughed and I smiled. I was very quiet that afternoon. After the introduction, everyone went about his or her business. I was left with my aunt and uncle, and we sat on the verandah. I loved the view from the house and kept looking toward the city. Each time I turned to look at my uncle, he was smiling widely. My aunt continually brought us huge plates of rice, fish, stew, and plantains. She made me eat so much that my stomach became too big. After we had finished eating, my uncle showed me his carpentry tools and his worktable, which was outside, occupying most of the little yard.

"If you are interested in carpentry, I will be glad to have you as my apprentice. But knowing your father, I could probably guess that you want to go to school," my uncle said. I smiled and didn't say a word. Allie came back and asked Uncle if it was okay for me to go with him to a local soccer match. My uncle said only if I wanted to. I went with Allie down the street to a field in an area called Brookfields.

"I am happy that you will be staying with us, we can share my room," Allie said as we waited for the game to begin. He was older than I was and had finished secondary school. He was jovial and very disciplined. It showed in his manners. He spoke well and to the point.

Before the game started, a girl waved to us from the other side of the field. She had the most beautiful and open smile, and she was laughing a lot. I was about to ask who she was when Allie spoke. "She is our cousin, but she lives across the street with a foster family. Her name is Aminata. You will get to meet her." Aminata was the daughter of my father's second brother, who had a different mother. I later became closer to her and Allie than to the other children in my new family.

During my many walks with my uncle, I learned that my grandfather had many wives and that my father had brothers he never talked about. My father was the only child from his mother's side.

At the soccer match, all I could think about was the discovery of a family I never thought existed. I was happy, but I had become accustomed to not showing it. Allie laughed throughout the game, and I couldn't even get myself to smile. When we returned, my uncle was on the verandah, waiting to take me back to the center. He held my hand as we walked to the bus station. I was quiet the entire trip. I spoke only to thank my uncle after he had given me transportation money to use if I decided to visit on my own. At the entrance of the center, my uncle hugged me, and as we parted, he turned around and said, "I'll see you soon again, my son."

19

Two weeks earlier, Leslie had told me that I was to be "repatri-ated" and reinstated into normal society. I was to live with my uncle. Those two weeks felt longer than the eight months I had spent at Benin Home. I was worried about living with a family. I had been on my own for years and had taken care of myself without any guidance from anyone. I was afraid that I might look ungrateful to my uncle, who didn't have to take me in, if I distanced myself from the family unit. I was worried about what to do when my nightmares and mi-graines took hold of me. How was I going to explain my sadness, which I am unable to hide as it takes over my face, to my new family, especially the children? I didn't have answers to these questions, and when I told Esther about them, she told me that everything was going to be fine, but I wanted more than just a reassurance.

I lay in my bed night after night staring at the ceiling and thinking, Why have I survived the war? Why was I the last person in my imme-diate family to be alive? I didn't know. I stopped playing soccer and table tennis. I went to see Esther every day, though, and would say hello, ask how she was, and then get lost in my own head thinking about what life was going to be like after the center. Sometimes Esther would have to snap her fingers in front of my face to bring me back. At night, I quietly sat on the verandah with Mohamed, Alhaji, and Mambu. I wouldn't notice when they left the bench that we all sat on.

When the day of my repatriation finally came, I packed my few belongings in a plastic bag. I had a pair of sneakers, four T-shirts, three shorts, toothpaste, a toothbrush, a bottle of Vaseline lotion, a Walkman and some cassettes, two long-sleeved shirts, and two pairs of pants and a tie—these had been bought for me to wear for my conference talks. I waited, my heart beating faster, the way it had when my mother dropped me off for the first time at a boarding school. The van was heard galloping on the gravel road, making its way to the center. Picking up my plastic bag, I walked to the hospital building where I was to wait. Mohamed, Alhaji, and Mambu were sitting on the front steps, and Esther emerged, smiling. The van made a turn and halted at the side of the road. It was late afternoon, the sky was still blue, but the sun was dull, hiding behind the only cloud. Leslie sat in the front seat and waited for me to board, so he could take me to my new home.

"I have to go," I said to everyone, my voice shaking. I extended my hand to Mohamed, but instead of shaking it, he leapt up and hugged me. Mambu embraced me while Mohamed was still holding me. He squeezed me hard, as if he knew it was goodbye forever. (After I left the center, Mambu went back to the front lines, because his family refused to take him in.) At the end of the hug, Alhaji shook hands with me. We squeezed each other's hand and stared into each other's eyes, remembering all that we had been through. I tapped him on the shoulder and he smiled, as he understood that I was saying we were going to be fine. I never saw him again, since he continually moved from one foster home to another. At the end of our handshake, Alhaji stepped back, saluted me, and whispered, "Goodbye, squad leader." I tapped him on the shoulder again; I couldn't salute him in return. Esther stepped forward, her eyes watery. She hugged me tighter than she ever had. I didn't return her hug very well, as I was busy trying to hold back my tears. After she let go, she gave me a piece of paper. "This is my address. Come by anytime," she said.

I went to Esther's home several weeks after that. My timing wasn't good, as she was on her way to work. She hugged me, and this time I squeezed back; this made her laugh after we stood apart. She looked me straight in the eyes. "Come and see me next weekend so we can have more time to catch up, okay?" she said. She was wearing her white uniform and was on her way to take on other traumatized children. It must be tough living with so many war stories. I was just living with one, mine, and it was difficult, as the nightmares about what had happened continued to torment me. Why does she do it? Why do they all do it? I thought as we went our separate ways. It was the last time I saw her. I loved her but never told her.

My uncle picked me up in his arms as soon as I got off the van and carried me onto the verandah. "I welcome you today like a chief. Your feet may touch the ground when you lose your chieftaincy, which begins now," my uncle said, laughing, as he set me down. I smiled but was nervous. My four cousins—Allie and the three girls, Matilda, Kona, and Sombo—took turns hugging me, their faces bright with smiles.

"You must be hungry; I cooked you a welcome home *sackie thomboi*," my aunt said. She had made cassava leaves with chicken just to welcome me. To have chicken prepared for anyone was a rarity, and it was considered an honor. People ate chicken only on holidays like Christmas or New Year's. Auntie Sallay held my hand and made me sit on a bench next to my uncle. She brought the food out, and my uncle and I ate together from the same plate with our hands. It was a good meal and I licked my fingers, enjoying the rich palm oil. My uncle looked at me, laughing, and said to his wife, "Sallay, you have done it again. This one is here to stay."

After we washed our hands, my cousin Allie, twenty-one years old, was called to the verandah and asked to show me where I was to sleep. I took my plastic bag and followed him to another house that was behind the one with my uncle's bedroom. The passageway between the houses was like a pathway with stones carefully placed on each side of the walkway.

Allie held the door for me as I entered the clean, organized room. The bed was made, the clothes that hung on a post were ironed, the shoes were properly lined on a rack, and the brown tile floor was shiny. He pulled a mattress from under the bed and explained to me that I would sleep on the floor, as he and his roommate shared the bed. I was to fold the mattress and put it back under the bed every morning. After he was done explaining how I could contribute to keeping the room clean and in order, I went back to the verandah and sat with my uncle. He put his arm around me and pulled on my nose.

"Are you familiar with the city?" Uncle asked.

"Not really."

"Allie will take you around sometime, if you like. Or you can venture out there yourself, get lost, and find your way. It will be a good way to get to know the city." He chuckled. We heard a call for prayer that echoed throughout the city.

"I have to go for prayers. If you need anything, ask your cousins," he said, taking a kettle from the stoop and beginning to perform ablution. After he was done, he walked down the hill to a nearby mosque. My aunt came out of the room, tying her head with a cloth, and followed my uncle.

I sighed, sitting alone on the verandah. I was no longer nervous, but I missed Benin Home. Later that night, when my uncle and aunt returned from prayers, all my new family gathered around a cassette player on the verandah to listen to stories. My uncle rubbed his hands, pressed the play button, and a famous storyteller named Leleh Gbomba began telling a story about a man who had forgotten his heart at home when he went traveling around the world. I had heard the story in my grandmother's village when I was younger. My new family laughed throughout the telling of the story. I only smiled and was very quiet that night, as I was to be for a while more. But gradually I adjusted to being around people who were happy all the time.

A day or two after I had started living with my uncle, Allie gave me my first pair of dress shoes, a dress belt, and a stylish shirt.

"If you want to be a gentleman, you have to dress like one." He laughed. I was about to ask him why he had given me these things when he began to explain: "This is a secret. I want to take you to a dance tonight so you can enjoy yourself. We will leave after Uncle goes to bed."

That night we snuck out and went dancing at a pub. As Allie and I walked, I remembered when I used to go dancing back in secondary school with friends. It seemed so long ago, but I still recalled the different names of the dance nights: "Back to School," "Pens Down," "Bob Marley Night," and many more. We would dance until cock-crow, then take off our sweaty shirts, enjoying the cool morning breeze as we walked back to our dorms. I was truly happy back then.

"We are here," Allie said, shaking my hand and snapping his fingers. There were lots of young people waiting in line to get into the pub. The boys were well dressed, their pants ironed and shirts tucked in. The girls wore beautiful flowered dresses and high heels that made them taller than some of the boys they were with. Their lips were also painted with bright colors. Allie was excited and he chatted with the people in front of us. I was quiet, looking at the different colored lights that hung at the entrance. There was one big blue light that made people's white shirts especially beautiful. We finally made it to the entrance and Allie paid for the two of us. The music was extremely loud inside, but then again, I had not been to a pub for many years. I followed Allie to the bar area, where we found a table and sat on two high stools.

"I am going to the dance floor," Allie announced, screaming so that I could hear him. He disappeared into the crowd. I sat for a while scoping out the place, and slowly began dancing by myself in the corner of the dance floor. Suddenly an extremely dark girl whose smile illuminated the dance floor pulled me and led me to the middle of the floor before I could resist. She started dancing close to me. I looked back at Allie, who was standing at the bar. He gave me a thumbs-up, and I began to move slowly until the rhythm took over. I danced one *raggamorphy* song with the girl, and then there was a slow jam. She pulled me toward her and I held her hand delicately as we swayed to the music. I could feel her heart beat. She tried to catch my eyes, but I looked away. In the middle of the song, some older boy pulled her away from me. She waved as she was being escorted through the crowd and toward the door.

"You are smooth, man. I saw that." Allie was now standing next to me. He began walking toward the bar, and I followed him. We leaned against the counter, facing the dance floor. He was still smiling.

"I really didn't do anything. She just wanted to dance with me and I couldn't say no," I said.

"Exactly, you say nothing and the women come to you," he teased. I didn't want to talk anymore. A memory of a town we had attacked during a school dance had been triggered. I could hear the terrified cries of teachers and students, could see the blood cover the dance floor. Allie tapped me on the shoulder and brought me back to the present. I smiled at him, but I was deeply sad for the rest of our stay. We danced all night and returned before Uncle woke up.

A few nights later, I returned to the pub alone and saw the same girl. She told me her name was Zainab.

"Sorry about last time," she said. "My brother wanted to go home and I had to go with him, otherwise my parents would have gotten worried."

Like me, she was alone this night.

I dated her for three weeks, but then she began to ask too many questions. Where was I from? What was it like growing up *upline*? *Upline* is a Krio word mostly used in Freetown to refer to the back-wardness of the inner country, its inhabitants, and their mannerisms. I was unwilling to tell her anything, so she broke it off. That was the story of my relationship with girls in Freetown. They wanted to know about me, and I wasn't ready to tell them. It was okay. I liked being alone.

Leslie came to see me. He asked how I was doing and what I had been up to. I wanted to tell him that I had had one severe migraine wherein the image of a burning village flashed in my mind, followed by wail-ings of many voices; that I had felt the back of my neck tighten and my head become heavy, as if a huge rock had been placed on it. Instead, I told him only that everything was fine. Leslie pulled out a pad and began writing something on it. When he was done he turned to me and said, "I have a proposition for you. It is important."

"Always the bearer of news, aren't you?" I joked.

"This is important." He studied the pad he held in his hand and continued. "There is an interview for two children to be sent to the United Nations in New York, in America, to talk about the lives of children in Sierra Leone and what can be done about it. Mr. Kamara, the director of your former rehabilitation center, recommended that you go for the interview. Here is the address, if you are interested." He tore the paper off and handed it to me. As I was looking at it, he went on: "If you want me to go with you, come by the office. Dress up for the interview, okay?" He searched my face for an answer. I didn't say anything. Afterward, he left with a smile on his face that said he knew I would show up for the interview.

The day of the interview finally arrived, and I dressed casually for it. I wore sneakers, nice black pants, and a green long-sleeved shirt. I tucked my shirt in as I walked down to Siaka Stevens Street to the address that Leslie had given me. I told no one where I was going. I had wanted to talk to Allie about it, but hesitated, because I knew that if I did, I would have to tell him more than he knew about me, more than my uncle had told him.

It was almost midday, but the tar road was already too hot. I watched a flying plastic bag land on the road and immediately begin to melt. *Poda podas* went by, their apprentices shouting the names of their destinations to attract customers. A few feet ahead a vehicle had stopped on the side of the street and the driver was pouring water from a jerrican into its overheated engine. "This car drinks more water than a cow," he grumbled. I was walking slowly, but my undershirt got soaked with sweat.

When I arrived at the address, I stood in front of the tall building and marveled at its height before entering. In the lobby there were about twenty boys, all dressed better than I. Their parents were giving them last-minute points for the interview. I studied the big cement columns in the building. I liked thinking about how people had managed to create and erect such large cement pillars. I was busy examining one pillar when a man tapped me on the shoulder and asked if I was there for the interview. I nodded, and he pointed to the open metal box that all the boys now stood in. I hesitantly walked into the congested box and the boys laughed at me, as I stood there unaware that I had to press the button for the box to start moving. I had never been in a box like this before. Where was it taking us? A boy in a blue shirt squeezed his way past me and pressed the number 5 button. It lit up, and the box closed on us. I looked about me and saw that everyone was calm, so I knew that there was no need to worry. The box began to move up, fast. The other boys remained calm, adjusting their ties and shirts. When the doors opened, I was the last to step out into a large open room with brown leather couches. There was a man sitting at the desk at the far wall and he motioned for me to find a place to sit. The other boys had already seated themselves. I sat away from them and looked about the room. Through the window I could see the tops of other buildings, and I decided to get up and look around to see how high up from the ground we were. As I was making my way to the window, my name was called.

A really light-skinned man (I couldn't tell if he was Sierra Leonean or not) sat in a big black leather chair. "Please have a seat and I will be with you in a moment," he said in English, and he shuffled through some papers, picked up a phone, and dialed a number. When the person picked up on the other end, the man just said, "It is a go-ahead," and hung up.

He turned toward me and eyed me for a bit before he began to question me, speaking very slowly, in English.

"What is your name?" he asked, looking at the list of names on his desk.

"Ishmael," I said, and he checked my name before I could tell him my last name.

"Why do you think you should go to the UN to present the situation affecting children in this country?" He raised his head from the list and looked at me.

"Well, I am from the part of the country where I have not only suffered because of the war but I have also participated in it and undergone rehabilitation. So I have a better understanding, based on my experience of the situation, than any of these city boys who are here for the interview. What are they going to say when they go over there? They don't know anything about the war except the news of it." I looked at the man, who was smiling, and it made me a bit angry.

"What else do you have to say?" he asked.

"Nothing, except that I am wondering why you are smiling." I sat back in the soft leather chair.

"You can go now," the man said, still smiling.

I got up and left the room, leaving the door open behind me. I walked toward the box and stood by it. I stood there and waited for several minutes, but nothing happened. I didn't know what to do to make the box come upstairs. The boys who were waiting for the interview began to laugh. Then the man who sat behind the desk walked toward me and pushed a button on the wall. The doors immediately opened and I walked in. The man pressed the number 1 button and waved to me as the doors closed. I tried to find something to hold on to, but the box was already at street level. I walked out of the building and stood outside examining its structure. I have to tell Mohamed about the inside of this marvelous building when I see him, I thought.

I walked home slowly that afternoon, watching the cars go by. I didn't think much about the interview except that I still wondered why the man who had interviewed me had smiled. I meant what I said and it was not a funny matter. At some point during my walk, a convoy of cars, military vans, and Mercedes-Benzes festooned with national flags passed by. Their windows were tinted, so I couldn't see who rode in them, and they were too fast, anyway. When I got home, I asked Allie if he knew of a powerful man who parades the city in such a way. He told me that it was Tejan Kabbah, the new president, who had won the election under the banner of the Sierra Leone Peoples Party (SLPP) in March 1996, eight months earlier. I had never heard of this man.

That night my uncle brought home a bag of groundnut. Auntie Sallay boiled the groundnut and put it out on a large tray. All of us, my uncle, his wife, Allie, Kona, Matilda, Sombo, and I, sat around the tray and ate the groundnut, listening to another recording of Leleh Gbomba's. He was telling a story about how he became friends with another boy before they were born. Their mothers were neighbors and were pregnant at the same time, so the two of them met while they were still in their mothers' bellies. The storyteller vividly described the landscape of their pre-infant life: the hunting they did, the games they played, how they listened to our world . . . It was a very funny story that took shockingly impossible twists and turns and left us in awe. My uncle, aunt, and cousins laughed so hard that they couldn't stop for hours, even after the story had ended. I began to laugh, too, because my uncle was trying to say something and he was so possessed with laughter that he couldn't say a complete word without launching into another fit of laughter. "We should do this again. Laughing like this is good for the soul," my uncle said, still laughing a little. We wished one another a good night and went to our different sleeping places.

One morning Mr. Kamara turned up at my uncle's house in the Children Associated with the War (CAW) van. He had told me I had been chosen to go to the UN a few days before, but I had only told Mohamed about this, as I didn't actually believe that I was going to travel to New York City. It was before midday when Mr. Kamara arrived and my uncle had left for work. My aunt was in the kitchen; the look on her face told me that my uncle would learn about Mr. Kamara's visit. I knew then that I would have to tell my uncle about the trip.

"Good morning," Mr. Kamara said, checking his watch to make sure it was still morning.

"Good morning," I replied.

"Are you ready to go to town and begin preparation for the trip?" he asked in English. Since Mr. Kamara had found out that I had been chosen to go to the UN, he had spoken only English to me. I said goodbye to my aunt and jumped in the van, and we took off to get me a passport. It seemed as if everyone in the city had decided to get passports that day, perhaps preparing to leave the country. Luckily, Mr. Kamara had made an appointment, so we didn't have to wait in line. At the counter he presented my photo, the necessary forms, and the fee. A round-faced man carefully examined the documents and asked for my birth certificate. "You have to show me proof that you were born in this country," the man said. I became really upset and almost slapped the man, who insisted that I must present proof of birth in Sierra Leone even after I had told him that no one had the chance to assemble documents of that nature when the war reached them. He was naïve about the reality I was trying to explain to him. Mr. Kamara pulled me aside and gently asked me to sit on a bench while he chatted with the man. Eventually he demanded to see his boss. After hours of waiting, someone was able to dig up a copy of my birth certificate, and they told Mr. Kamara to come back for the passport in four days.

"The first step is completed. Now we will have to get you the visa," Mr. Kamara said as we walked out of the passport office. I didn't reply, because I was still upset, exhausted, and just wanted to go home.

My uncle was home when I was dropped off that evening. When I greeted him, he had a smile on his face that said, "Tell me what is going on." I did. I told him that I was to go to the United Nations in New York City and talk about the war, as it relates to children. My uncle didn't believe it. "People are always lying to others with such promises. Don't let them get your hopes up, my son," he said.

Every morning before he left for work, he would say jokingly, "So what are we doing today in planning to go to America?"

Mr. Kamara took me shopping. He bought me a suitcase and some clothes, mostly long-sleeved shirts, dress pants, and traditionally waxed, colorful cotton suits with intricate embroidery on the collars, sleeves, and hems of pants. I showed these things to my uncle, but still he didn't believe that I would be going on the trip.

"Maybe they just want to give you a new look, a more African look, instead of those big pants you always wear," he joked.

Sometimes my uncle and I went for strolls after work. He would ask how I was doing; I always told him I was fine. He would put his long arms around me and pull me closer. I felt he knew that I wanted to tell him certain things but couldn't find the right words. I hadn't told him that whenever I went to the bush with my cousins to fetch firewood, my mind would begin to wander to things I had seen and done in the past. Standing next to a tree with red frozen sap on its bark would bring flashbacks of the many times we executed prisoners by tying them to trees and shooting them. Their blood stained the trees and never washed off, even during the rainy season. I hadn't told him that often I was reminded of what I had missed by watching the daily activities of families, a child hugging his father, holding his mother's wrap, or holding two parents' hands, swinging over gutters. It made me wish I could go back to the beginning and change things.

I had been told to meet a man by the name of Dr. Tamba at the American embassy on Monday morning. As I walked to the embassy, I listened to the gradual wakening of the city. The call for prayer from the central mosque echoed throughout the city, *poda podas* crowded the streets, their apprentices hanging on the open passenger doors and calling out the names of their destinations: "Lumley, Lumley" or "Congo Town . . ." It was still too early when I arrived, but there was already a long line of people waiting outside the embassy gates. Their faces were sad and filled with uncertainty, as if they awaited some trial that would determine whether they would die or stay alive. I didn't know what to do, so I stood in line. After an hour or so, Dr. Tamba arrived with another boy and asked me to follow him. He looked like a dignified man, so I guess we didn't have to wait in line. The other boy, who was also a former child soldier, introduced himself. "My name is Bah. I am happy to be going on this journey with you," he said, shaking my hand. I thought about what my uncle's reply would be to him: "Don't let them get your hopes up, young man."

We sat down on one of the few decent benches in a small open area in the embassy and waited for our interview. A white woman stood behind a transparent glass window; her voice came through the speakers underneath it. "What is the purpose of your visit to the United States?" she asked, never looking up from the papers before her.

When it was our turn, the woman behind the glass already had our passports. She didn't look at me; rather, she flipped through the pages of my new passport. I was very confused about why the window was set up in such a way that the human connection was lost between the interviewer and the interviewee.

"Speak into the microphone," she said, and she continued, "What is the purpose of your visit to the United States?"

"For a conference," I said.

"What is the conference about?"

"It is generally about issues affecting children around the world," I explained.

"And where is this conference?"

"At the UN in New York City."

"Do you have any guarantee that you will come back to your home country?" I was thinking, when she continued, "Do you have any property, a bank account that will guarantee your return?"

I frowned. Do you know anything about people's lives in this country? I thought of asking her. If she could only look at me directly, perhaps she wouldn't have asked the last two questions. No one my age in my country has a bank account or even dreams of having one, much less property to declare. Mr. Tamba told her that he was the CAW chaperon going on the trip with us and that he would make sure that we returned to Sierra Leone at the end of the conference.

The woman asked me the final question: "Do you know anyone in the United States?"

"No, I have never been anywhere out of this country, and this is actually my first time in this city," I told her. She closed my passport and put it aside. "Come back at four-thirty."

Outside, Dr. Tamba told us that we had gotten the visas and that he would pick up the passports and hold on to them until the day of our departure. It had finally begun to look as if we were going to travel, even though I had seen my passport only at a glance.

I held my suitcase in my right hand and was wearing brown traditional summer pants with zigzag thread patterns at the bottom and a T-shirt. My uncle was sitting on the verandah when I came from Allie's room.

"I am on my way to the airport," I said, smiling, as I knew my uncle was going to be sarcastic.

"Sure. Give me a call when you get to America. Well, I don't have a phone, so call Aminata's house and she can come and get me." My uncle giggled.

"Okay, I will," I said, giggling as well.

"Ah, children, come and say goodbye to your brother. I do not know where he is going, but he needs our blessings," my uncle said. Matilda, Kona, and Sombo came to the verandah holding buckets in their hands. They were on their way to fetch water. They hugged me and wished me luck on my journey. My aunt came out of the kitchen smelling of smoke and hugged me. "Wherever you are going, you will need to smell like your home. This is my perfume to you." She giggled and stepped back. My uncle stood up and hugged me, put his arm around my shoulder and said, "My good wishes are with you. So I will see you later for dinner, then." He went back to sit in his chair on the verandah.

20

MY CONCEPTION OF NEW YORK CITY came from rap music. I envisioned it as a place where people shot each other on the street and got away with it; no one walked on the streets, rather people drove in their sports cars looking for nightclubs and for violence. I really wasn't looking forward to being somewhere this crazy. I had had enough of that back home.

It was dark when the plane landed at John F. Kennedy International Airport. It was 4:30 p.m. I asked Dr. Tamba why it was dark so early in this country. "Because it is winter," he said. "Oh!" I nodded, but the early darkness still didn't make sense to me. I knew the word "winter" from Shakespeare's texts and I thought I should look up its meaning again.

Dr. Tamba took our passports and did all the talking at immigration. We got our bags and headed toward the sliding doors. Maybe we shouldn't just venture into the streets like that, I thought, but Dr. Tamba was already outside. When Bah and I stepped through the sliding doors, we were greeted by an extremely cold wind. I felt my skin tighten, I couldn't feel my face, and it seemed my ears had fallen off; my fingers hurt, and my teeth chattered. The wind penetrated through the summer pants and T-shirt I was wearing, and it felt as though I wasn't wearing anything. I was shivering as I ran back into the terminal. I had never in my life felt this cold. How can anyone survive in this country? I thought, rubbing my hands together and jumping around to generate some heat. Bah stood outside with Dr. Tamba, his hands wrapped around himself and shaking uncontrollably. For some reason, Dr. Tamba had a jacket but Bah and I didn't. I waited in the terminal while Dr. Tamba hailed a taxi, then I ran outside and jumped in, quickly closing the door behind me. There were little white things falling out of the sky, and they seemed to be accumulating on the ground. What is this white stuff falling from the sky? I thought to myself. Dr. Tamba told the driver our destination, reading it off a piece of paper he held in his hand.

"Is this your first time in the city, and are you guys enjoying the beautiful snowfall?" the taxi driver asked.

"Yes, it is their first time in the city," Dr. Tamba replied, and busied himself putting away our documents. I had never heard of the word "snow" before. It is not exactly something that we discuss in Sierra Leone. But I had seen movies about Christmas, and this white fluffy stuff was in those movies. It must be Christmas here every day, I thought.

When we entered the city, it seemed as if someone had lit the many tall buildings that shot into the sky. From afar, some of the buildings looked as if they were made of colorful lights. The city glittered, and I was so completely overwhelmed that I couldn't decide where to look. I thought I had seen tall buildings in Freetown, but these were beyond tall, it seemed they were poking the sky. There were so many cars on the street, and they impatiently honked, even when the light was red. And then I saw people walking on the sidewalks. I rubbed my eyes to make sure that I was really seeing people on the streets of New York City. It wasn't as dangerous as I had heard it was. Not so far. The lights were brighter than the ones back home, and I kept looking for the utility poles that the electric wires hung on, but I couldn't see any.

We arrived at the Vanderbilt YMCA hotel on Forty-seventh Street and entered the lobby holding our luggage. We followed Dr. Tamba to the front desk and got our room keys. I had a room to myself for the first time in my life. To top that, I had a television, which I watched all night long. It was really hot in the room, so I took my clothes off and sweated in front of the television. Two days later I learned that the reason the room was so hot was that the radiator was on full blast. I didn't know what it looked like, least of all how to turn the heat down or off. I remember thinking about the strangeness of this country: it is very cold outside and extremely hot inside.

On the morning following our arrival, I went downstairs to the cafeteria, where fifty-seven children from twenty-three countries were waiting to have breakfast and to begin the United Nations First International Children's Parliament. There were children from Lebanon, Cambodia, Kosovo, Brazil, Norway, Yemen, Mozambique, Palestine, Guatemala, the U.S. (New York), South Africa, Peru, Northern Ireland, India, Papua New Guinea, Malawi, to name a few. While I was looking around for Bah and Dr. Tamba, a white woman pulled me to the side and introduced herself.

"My name is Kristen. I am from Norway." She extended her hand.

"I am Ishmael from Sierra Leone." I shook her hand, and she opened an envelope of name tags and placed one on my shirt. She smiled and motioned for me to join the breakfast line as she walked away, looking for other children without name tags. I followed behind two boys who were speaking a strange language. They knew what they wanted, but I had no idea what to get or what the names of the foods were that the cooks were making. Throughout my stay, I was baffled by the food. I would simply order "the same thing," or put on my plate whatever I'd seen others put on theirs. Sometimes I was lucky to like what landed there. That was usually not the case. I asked Dr. Tamba if he knew where we could get some rice and fish stew in palm oil, some cassava leaves or okra soup. He smiled and said, "When you are in Rome, you do as the Romans do."

I should have brought my own food from home to hold me until I learn about the food in this country, I thought as I drank my glass of orange juice.

After breakfast we walked two blocks in the freezing weather down

to a building where most of the meetings took place. It was still snow-
ing outside, and I was wearing summer dress pants and a long-sleeved
shirt. I told myself that I wouldn't want to live in such an unpleasantly
cold country, where I would always have to worry about my nose, ears,
and face falling off.

That first morning in New York City, we learned about each other's lives
for hours. Some of the children had risked their life to attend the conference. Others had walked hundreds of miles to neighboring countries to be able to get on a plane. Within minutes of talking to each
other, we knew that the room was filled with young people who had
had a very difficult childhood, and some were going to return to these
lives at the end of the conference. After the introductions, we sat in a
circle so that the different facilitators could tell us about themselves.

Most of the facilitators worked for NGOs, but there was a short
white woman with long dark hair and bright eyes who said, "I am a
storyteller." I was surprised at this and gave her all my attention. She
used elaborate gestures and spoke very clearly, enunciating every word.
She said her name was Laura Simms. She introduced her co-facilitator,
Therese Plair, who was light-skinned, had African features, and held a
drum. Before Laura finished talking, I had already decided that I
would take her workshop. She said she would teach us how to tell our
stories in a more compelling way. I was curious to find out how this
white woman, born in New York City, had become a storyteller.

That same morning Laura kept looking at Bah and me. I didn't
know that she had noticed we were wearing only our light African
shirts and pants and sat closer to the radiators, our hands wrapped
around our tiny bodies, and every now and then shaking from the cold
that seemed to have settled in our bones. In the afternoon before
lunch, she approached us. "Do you have winter jackets?" she asked.
We shook our heads. A painful concern passed over her face, making
her smile look forced. That evening she returned with winter jackets,
hats, and gloves for us. I felt I was wearing a heavy green costume that
made my body bigger than it looked. But I was happy, because now I

could venture outside to see the city after the daily workshops. Years later, when Laura offered me one of her winter jackets, I refused to accept it because it was a woman's jacket. She joked with me about the fact that when she had first met me I was so cold that I didn't care that I was wearing a woman's winter jacket.

Bah and I became a little close with Laura and Therese over the course of the conference. Sometimes Laura would talk to us about stories I had heard as a child. I was in awe of the fact that a white woman from across the Atlantic Ocean, who had never been to my country, knew stories so specific to my tribe and upbringing. When she became my mother years later, she and I would always talk about whether it was destined or coincidental that I came from a very storytelling-oriented culture to live with a mother in New York who is a storyteller.

I called my uncle in Freetown during my second day. Aminata answered the phone.

"Hi. This is Ishmael. Could I please speak to Uncle?" I asked.

"I will go get him. Call back in two minutes." Aminata hung up the phone. When I called back, my uncle picked up.

"I am in New York City," I told him.

"Well," he said, "I guess I believe you, because I haven't seen you in a few days." He giggled. I opened the hotel window to let him hear the sounds of New York.

"That doesn't sound like Freetown," he said, and was silent for a bit before he continued. "So what is it like?"

"It is excruciatingly cold," I said, and he began to laugh.

"Ah! Maybe it is your initiation to the white people's world. Well, tell me all about it when you return. Stay inside if you have to." As he spoke, I pictured the dusty gravel road by his house. I could smell my aunt's groundnut soup.

Every morning we would quickly walk through the snow to a conference room down the street. There we would cast our sufferings aside and intelligently discuss solutions to the problems facing children in our various countries. At the end of these long discussions, our faces and eyes glittered with hope and the promise of happiness. It seemed we were transforming our sufferings as we talked about ways to solve their causes and let them be known to the world.

On the night of the second day, Madoka from Malawi and I walked west along Forty-seventh Street without realizing we were heading straight into the heart of Times Square. We were busy looking at the buildings and all the people hurrying by when we suddenly saw lights all over the place and shows playing on huge screens. We looked at each other in awe of how absolutely amazing and crowded the place was. One of the screens had a woman and a man in their underwear; I guess they were showing it off. Madoka pointed at the screen and laughed. Others had music videos or numbers going across. Everything flashed and changed very quickly. We stood at the corner for a while, mesmerized by the displays. After we were able to tear our eyes away from them, we walked up and down Broadway for hours, staring at the store windows. I didn't feel cold, as the number of people, the glittering buildings, and the sounds of cars overwhelmed and intrigued me. I thought I was dreaming. When we returned to the hotel later that night, we told the other children about what we had seen. After that, we all went out to Times Square every evening.

Madoka and I had wandered off to a few places in the city before our scheduled sightseeing days. We had been to Rockefeller Plaza, where we saw a huge decorated Christmas tree, statues of angels, and the people ice-skating. They kept going around and around, and Madoka and I couldn't understand why they enjoyed this. We had also gone to the World Trade Center with Mr. Wright, a Canadian man we had met at the hotel. One evening, when the fifty-seven of us got on the subway on our way to the South Street Seaport, I asked Madoka, "How come everyone is so quiet?" He looked around the train and replied, "It is not the same as public transportation back home." Shantha, the cameraperson for the event, who later became my aunt when I returned to live in New York, pointed the camera at us, and Madoka and I posed for her. On every trip I would make mental notes on things I needed to tell my uncle, cousins, and Mohamed. I didn't think they would believe any of it.

On the last day of the conference, a child from each country spoke briefly at the UN Economic and Social Council (ECOSOC) chamber about their country and experiences. There were diplomats and all sorts of influential people. They wore suits and ties and sat upright listening to us. I proudly sat behind the Sierra Leone name plaque, listening and waiting for my turn to speak. I had a speech that had been written for me in Freetown, but I decided to speak from my heart, instead. I talked briefly about my experience and my hope that the war would end—it was the only way that adults would stop recruiting children. I began by saying, "I am from Sierra Leone, and the problem that is affecting us children is the war that forces us to run away from our homes, lose our families, and aimlessly roam the forests. As a result, we get involved in the conflict as soldiers, carriers of loads, and in many other difficult tasks. All this is because of starvation, the loss of our families, and the need to feel safe and be part of something when all else has broken down. I joined the army really because of the loss of my family and starvation. I wanted to avenge the deaths of my family. I also had to get some food to survive, and the only way to do that was to be part of the army. It was not easy being a soldier, but we just had to do it. I have been rehabilitated now, so don't be afraid of me. I am not a soldier anymore; I am a child. We are all brothers and sisters. What I have learned from my experiences is that revenge is not good. I joined the army to avenge the deaths of my family and to survive, but I've come to learn that if I am going to take revenge, in that process I will kill another person whose family will want revenge; then revenge and revenge and revenge will never come to an end . . ."

After all our presentations, we sang a chant we had come up with. Then we began to sing other songs; we cried, we laughed, and we danced. It was an exceptionally moving afternoon. We were all sad to leave each other, as we had learned that we were not returning to peaceful places. Madoka and I put our arms around each other and jumped around to the music. Bah was dancing with another group of boys. Dr. Tamba sat in the audience smiling for the first time since we had arrived in New York City. After the dance, Laura pulled me aside and told me that she was moved by what I had said.

That night we went out to an Indian restaurant, and I was happy that someone in this part of the world serves rice. We ate a lot, chatted, exchanged addresses, and then went to Laura's house in the East Village. I couldn't understand why she called the area a village, because it didn't look like any village I knew. Our chaperons didn't come with us; they went back to the hotel. I didn't know that Laura's house was going to be my future home. There were traditionally woven cloths from all over the world hanging on the walls; statues of animals sat on large bookshelves that contained storybooks; clay vases with beautiful and exotic birds on them stood on tables; and there were bamboo instruments and other strange ones. The house was big enough to hold all fifty-seven of us. First, we sat around in Laura's living room and told stories; then we danced into the night. It was our last night in New York and it was the perfect place to spend it, because the house was as interesting and filled with amazing stories as our group was. Everyone felt comfortable and saw something from their home. Being in the house felt as though we had left New York City and entered a different world.

The next evening, Laura and Shantha accompanied Bah, Dr. Tamba, and me to the airport. At first we were all quiet in the car, but gradually we all, except Dr. Tamba, began to sob. At the terminal the sobbing intensified as we said goodbye, hugging each other. Laura and Shantha gave us their addresses and telephone numbers so that we could keep in touch. We left New York City on November 15, 1996. My sixteenth birthday was eight days away, and throughout the flight back home I still felt as if I was dreaming, a dream that I didn't want to wake up from. I was sad to leave, but I was also pleased to have met people outside of Sierra Leone. Because if I was to get killed upon my return, I knew that a memory of my existence was alive somewhere in the world.

21

SOME EVENINGS I told my family (including Mohamed, who now lived with us) stories about my trip. I described everything to them—the airfield, the airport, the plane, what it felt like to see clouds from the window of the plane. I would have a tingling sensation in my stomach as I remembered walking on a moving sidewalk in the Amsterdam airport. I had never seen so many white people, all hurriedly dragging their bags and running in different directions. I told them about the people I had met, the tall buildings of New York City, how people cursed on the street; I did my best to capture the snow and how it grew dark so early.

"It sounds like a strange trip," my uncle would remark. It felt, to me, like something that had all happened in my mind.

Mohamed and I started school again, at St. Edward's Secondary School. I was excited. I remembered the morning walks to my primary school; the sound of brooms sweeping fallen mango leaves, startling the birds, who would chatter in even higher pitches as if inquiring from each other the meaning of the harsh sound. My school had only a small building, which was made of mud bricks and a tin roof. There were no doors, no cement on the floor inside, and it was too small to hold all the pupils. Most of my classes were conducted outside under mango trees that provided shade.

Mohamed mostly remembered the lack of school materials in our primary and secondary schools, and how we had to help the teachers grow crops in their farms or gardens. It was the only way the teachers, who hadn't been paid for years, could make a living. The more we talked about it, the more I realized that I had forgotten what it felt like to be a student, to sit in class, to take notes, do homework, make friends, and provoke other students. I was eager to return. But on the first day of school in Freetown, all the students sat apart from us, as if Mohamed and I were going to snap any minute and kill someone. Somehow they had learned that we had been child soldiers. We had not only lost our childhood in the war but our lives had been tainted by the same experiences that still caused us great pain and sadness.

We always walked to school slowly. I liked it because I was able to think about where my life was going. I was confident that nothing could get any worse than it had been, and that thought made me smile a lot. I was still getting used to being part of a family again. I also began telling people that Mohamed was my brother, so that I wouldn't have to explain anything. I knew I could never forget my past, but I wanted to stop talking about it so that I would be fully present in my new life.

As usual, I had gotten up early in the morning, and I was sitting on the flat stone behind the house waiting for the city to wake up. It was May 25, 1997. But instead of the usual sounds that brought the city to life, it was woken that morning by gunshots erupting around the State House and the House of Parliament. The gunshots woke everyone, and I joined my uncle and neighbors on the verandah. We didn't know what was going on, but we could see soldiers running along Pademba Road and army trucks speeding up and down in front of the prison area.

The gunshots increased throughout the day, spreading across the city. The city folks stood outside on their verandahs, tensed up, shaking with fear. Mohamed and I looked at each other: "Not again." By early afternoon the central prison had been opened and the prisoners set free. The new government handed them guns as they got out. Some went straight to the houses of the judges and lawyers who had sentenced them, killing them and their families or burning their houses if they were not around. Others joined the soldiers, who had started looting shops. The smoke from the burning houses filled the air, draping the city in fog.

Someone came on the radio and announced himself as the new president of Sierra Leone. His name, he said, was Johnny Paul Koroma, and he was leader of the Armed Forces Revolutionary Council (AFRC), which had been formed by a group of Sierra Leone Army (SLA) officers to overthrow the democratically elected President Tejan Kabbah. Koroma's English was as bad as the reason he gave for the coup. He advised everyone to go to work by saying that everything was in order. In the background of his speech, gunshots and angry soldiers, cursing and jubilating, almost drowned him out.

Later in the night another announcement came over the radio, this one declaring that the rebels (RUF) and the army had collaborated in ousting the civilian government "for the benefit of the nation." Rebels and soldiers on the front lines started pouring into the city. The entire nation crumbled into a state of lawlessness. I hated what was happening. I couldn't return to my previous life. I didn't think I could make it out alive this time.

The AFRC/RUF, "Sobels," as they were called, had begun blowing up bank vaults using RPGs and other explosives and looting the money. Sometimes the Sobels halted people as they walked by, searched them, and took whatever they could find. They occupied the secondary schools and university campuses. There was nothing to do during the day except sit on the verandah. Uncle decided to finish building a house we had been working on since I came to live with him. In the morning we walked up to the land and worked until the early-afternoon gunshots sent us running back home to take cover under beds. But day by day, it got too dangerous to be in the open, as stray bullets had killed many people. So before long we stopped working on it.

Armed men had forcefully taken most of the food in the city from shops and markets, and imports of food from outside the country and from the provinces to the city had been stopped. What little was left had to be sought in the midst of the madness. Laura Simms had been sending me money and I had saved some of it, so Mohamed and I decided to go to town to try and buy some *gari*, cans of sardines, rice, anything we could find. I knew that I would risk running into my former military friends, who would kill me if I told them I wasn't part of the war anymore. But at the same time I couldn't just stay home. I had to find food.

We had heard of a secret market in town conducted in a yard behind an abandoned house where otherwise unavailable food items were sold to civilians. They sold the items at twice the regular price, but the trip seemed worth the risk and expense. We headed out early in the morning, terrified of seeing someone we knew. We kept our heads down as we hurried past young rebels and soldiers. We arrived as the vendors were just beginning to put their food products out. We bought some rice, some palm oil, salt, and fish; by the time we were done, the market was filling up with people hurriedly trying to buy whatever they could afford.

As we were about to leave, an open Land Rover roared up and armed men jumped off before it came to a halt. They ran into the crowd of civilians, firing a warning shot. Over a megaphone the commander ordered everyone to put down their bags of food, put their hands behind their heads, and lie flat, facing the ground. A woman in the crowd panicked and decided to run. An armed man in a red headband shot her in the head. She screamed and fell, loudly hitting the stony ground. This caused more panic, and everyone scattered in different directions. We grabbed our goods and ran crouching. This was beginning to be too familiar.

While we were running away from the area, another Land Rover full of more armed men arrived, and they began firing and knocking people's heads with the butts of their guns. We hid behind a wall separating the marketplace and the main street, then kept to a fast but cautious path behind the houses off the bay. Almost at the end of the bay, where the tide slammed a sunken boat, we jumped on the main street with our goods tucked under our arms and began the final walk home. We were approaching the Cotton Tree at the center of town when we saw a group of protesters run by, holding posters that read STOP THE KILLING and the like. They wore white shirts and their heads were tied with white cloths. We tried to ignore them, but as we turned a corner to continue home, a group of armed men, half in civilian and half in military clothing, ran toward us, firing into the crowd. There was no way to break from the crowd, so we joined them. The armed men began tossing tear gas. Civilians began to vomit on the sidewalks and bleed through their noses. Everyone started running toward Kissy Street. It was impossible to breathe. I put my hand over my nose, which felt as if it had been dipped in hot spices. I held tight to the bag of food and ran with Mohamed, trying not to lose him in the crowd. Tears ran down my cheeks, and my eyeballs and eyelids felt heavy. I was getting furious, but I tried to contain myself, because I knew I couldn't afford to lose my temper. The result would be death, since I was now a civilian; I knew that.

We continued to run with the crowd, trying to find a way out and head home. My throat began to ache. Mohamed was coughing until the veins on his throat were visible. We managed to break free, and he put his head under the public pump. Suddenly another group of people came running toward us, as fast as they could. Soldiers were pursuing them, so we too began to charge ahead, still carrying our food.

We were now in the midst of student protesters on a street lined with tall buildings. A chopper that had been cycling above started to descend and move toward the crowd. Mohamed and I knew what was going to happen. We ran for the nearest gutter and dove in. The chopper swept down to street level. As soon as it was about twenty-five meters from the protesters, it spun around and faced them sideways. A soldier sitting in the open side opened fire with a machine gun, mowing down the crowd. People ran for their lives. The street that a minute before had been filled with banners and noise was now a silent graveyard full of restless souls fighting to reconcile their sudden deaths.

Mohamed and I ran head down through alleyways. We came to a

fence that faced a main street on which there was a roadblock. Armed men patrolled the area. We lay in the gutter for six hours, waiting for nightfall. Chances to escape death were better at night, because the red track of the bullets could be seen in the dark. There were others with us. One, a student in a blue T-shirt, had a sweaty face, and every few seconds he wiped his forehead with his shirt. A young woman, probably in her early twenties, sat with her head between her knees, trembling and rocking. Against the wall of the gutter, a bearded man whose shirt was stained with someone else's blood sat holding his head in his hands. I felt bad about what was happening, but was not as scared as these people, who had not experienced war before. It was their first time, and it was painful to watch them. I hoped that Uncle would not worry too much about our whereabouts. More gunshots and a cloud of tear gas floated by. We held our noses until the wind took the gas away. Nightfall seemed so far away, it felt like waiting for Judgment Day. But as it must, night finally came, and we made it home, crouching behind houses and jumping fences.

My uncle was sitting on the verandah, tears in his eyes. When I greeted him, he jumped up as if he had seen a ghost. He embraced us for a long time and told us not to go to the city anymore. But we had no choice. We would have to, in order to get food.

The gunshots didn't cease for the next five months; they became the new sound of the city. In the morning, families sat on their verandahs and held their children close, staring at the city streets where gunmen roamed in groups, looting, raping, and killing people at will. Mothers wrapped their trembling arms around their children each time the gunshots intensified. People mostly ate soaked raw rice with sugar or plain *gari* with salt, and listened to the radio, hoping to hear some good news. Sometimes during the day, there were several plumes of smoke rising from houses that had been set on fire by gunmen. We could hear them excitedly laughing at the sight of the burning houses. One evening, a neighbor who lived a few doors down from my uncle's house was listening to a pirate radio station that accused the new government of committing crimes against civilians. A few minutes later, a truck full of soldiers stopped in front of the man's house, dragged him, his wife, and his two older sons outside, shot them, and kicked their bodies into the nearby gutter. My uncle vomited after we had seen the act.

For the first three weeks people were so afraid that they didn't dare to leave their houses. But soon enough, everyone got used to the gunshots and the madness. People began going about their daily business of searching for food, even though stray bullets were likely to kill them. Children played guessing games, telling each other whether the gun fired was an AK-47, a G3, an RPG, or a machine gun. I mostly sat outside on the flat rock with Mohamed and we were both quiet. I was thinking about the fact that we had run so far away from the war, only to be caught back in it. There was nowhere to go from here.

I had lost contact with Laura in New York for more than five months. Before that, she and I had constantly written letters to each other. She would tell me what she was doing and ask that I take good care of myself. Her letters came from all over the world, where she had storytelling projects. Recently I had tried calling her collect every day, but was unsuccessful. The phones at Sierra-tel, the national telephone company, weren't going through anymore. Each day I sat on the verandah with my uncle and cousins looking toward the city. We had stopped listening to the storytelling cassette, as curfews started before dark. My uncle laughed less and less, and sighed more and more. We continued to hope that things would change, but they kept getting worse.

My uncle became sick. One morning we were sitting on the verandah when he complained he wasn't feeling very well. In the evening he developed a fever and he lay inside, groaning. Allie and I went to a nearby shop and bought medicine, but Uncle's fever grew worse day after day. Auntie Sallay would force him to eat, but he would vomit everything the moment she was done feeding him. All the hospitals and pharmacies were closed. We searched the city for doctors or nurses, but those who hadn't left would not leave their homes for fear they might not be able to return to their families again. One evening I was sitting by my uncle, wiping his forehead, when he fell off the bed.

I caught his long body in my arms and held his head on my lap. His cheekbones stood out of his round face. He looked at me and I could see in his eyes that he had given up hope. I begged him not to leave us. His lips were about to utter something, but they stopped shaking, and he was gone. I held him in my arms and thought about how I was going to break the news to his wife, who was boiling him some water in the kitchen. She came in soon afterward and dropped the hot water, splashing it on both of us. She refused to believe that her husband had died. I still held my uncle in my arms, tears running down my face. My entire body had gone numb. I couldn't move from where I sat. Mohamed and Allie came in and took Uncle away from me and put him on the bed. After a few minutes, I was able to get up. I went behind the house and punched the mango tree until Mohamed took me away from it. I was always losing everything that meant something to me.

My cousins cried, asking, Who is going to take care of us now? Why did this happen to us in these difficult times?

Down in the city, the gunmen fired off their guns.

My uncle was buried the next morning. Even in the midst of the madness, many people came for his burial. I walked behind the coffin, the sound of my footsteps clinging to my heart. I held hands with my cousins and Mohamed. My aunt had tried to come to the cemetery, but she collapsed right before we left the house. At the cemetery the imam read a few suras and my uncle was lowered into the hole and covered with mud. People quickly dispersed to continue their lives. I stayed behind with Mohamed. I sat on the ground next to the grave and talked to my uncle. I told him that I was sorry that we couldn't find him any help, that I hoped he knew that I really loved him and wished he could have been alive to see me as an adult. After I was done, I placed my hands on the heap of mud and quietly wept. I didn't realize how long I had been at the cemetery until after I had stopped crying. It was late in the evening and the curfew was about to begin. Mohamed and I ran as fast as we could back home before the soldiers started shooting.

A few days after my uncle was buried, I was finally able to make a collect call to Laura. I asked her if I could stay with her if I made my way to New York City. She said yes.

"No. I want you to really think about this. If I make my way to New York, can I stay with you at your house?" I asked again.

"Yes," she said again, and I told her that "I would visualize it" and would call her when I was in Conakry, the capital of Guinea, the one neighboring country that was peaceful and the only way out of Sierra Leone at that time. I had to leave, because I was afraid that if I stayed in Freetown any longer, I was going to end up being a soldier again or my former army friends would kill me if I refused. Some friends who had undergone rehabilitation with me had already rejoined the army.

I left Freetown early in the morning of the seventh day after my uncle passed away. I didn't tell anyone that I was leaving except Mohamed, who was to relay my departure to my aunt after she was done grieving. She had turned herself away from the world and everyone in it after Uncle's death. I left on October 31, 1997, while it was still a little dark outside. The curfew was still in place, but I needed to leave the city before the sun came out. It was less dangerous to travel at this hour, as some of the gunmen were dozing off and the night made it difficult for the militiamen to see me from afar. Gunshots echoed in the quiet city, and the morning breeze felt harsh against my face. The air smelled of rotten bodies and gunpowder. I shook hands with Mohamed. "I'll let you know where I end up," I told him. He tapped me on my shoulder and said nothing.

I had only a small dirty bag containing a few clothes. It was risky to travel with a big or fancy bag, as armed men would think that you were carrying something valuable and would possibly shoot you. As I walked into the last remains of the night, leaving Mohamed standing on the verandah, I became afraid. This was becoming too familiar. I stopped next to a utility pole for a bit, exhaled heavily, and threw some angry punches in the air. I have to try to get out, I thought, and if that doesn't work, then it is back to the army. I didn't like thinking this way.

I hurriedly walked near the gutters and took cover when I heard a vehicle approaching. I was the only civilian on the street, and I sometimes had to bypass checkpoints by either crawling in gutters or crouching behind houses. I safely made it to an old bus station that was no longer in use at the edge of the city. I was sweating and my eyelids trembled as I looked around the station. There were a lot of men—in their thirties, I presumed—some women, and a few families with children five years of age and older. They all stood in line against the dilapidated wall, some holding bundles of things and others their children's hands.

I walked to the back of the line and sat on my heels to make sure my money was still inside my sock, under my right foot. The man in front of me kept mumbling things to himself and pacing away from the wall and back. He was making me more nervous than I already was. After several minutes of quietly waiting, a man who had been standing in line with everyone else proclaimed himself the bus driver and asked everyone to follow him. We walked farther into the abandoned station, making our way over falling cement walls into an open area where we got on a bus, which was painted dark, even its rims, so that it would blend with the night. The bus rolled out of the station, its lights off, and took the back road out of the city. The road hadn't been used for years, so it seemed the bus was moving through bushes, as leaves and branches heavily slapped its side. It slowly galloped in the dark until the sun began to rise. At some point, we had to get off and walk behind it so that it would be able to climb a little hill. We were all very quiet, our faces tensed with fear, as we hadn't yet safely left the city area. We got back on the bus, and about an hour later it dropped us off at an old bridge.

We paid the driver and walked across the rusty bridge two at a time, and then had to walk all day to a junction where we waited for another bus that would arrive the next morning. This was the only way to get out of Freetown without being killed by the armed men and boys of the new government, who hated it when people left the city.

There were over thirty of us at the junction. We sat on the ground near the bushes and waited all night. No one said a word to one another, as we all knew that we hadn't completely escaped the madness. Parents whispered things in the ears of their children, afraid to let out their voices. Some people stared at the ground and others played with stones. Gunshots were faintly heard in the breeze. I sat at the edge of the gutter and chewed on some raw rice I had in a plastic bag. When will I stop running from this war? What if the bus doesn't show up? A neighbor in Freetown had told me about this only way out of the country. So far it seemed to be safe, but I was worried, as I knew how quickly things change for the worse in such circumstances.

I put the raw rice back into my bag and started walking down the dirt road to find a suitable place to sit for the night. There were people sleeping under the bushes near the bus stop. This way, they would be able to hear the bus if it pulled up during the night. Farther down, there were others clearing spaces under branches of plum trees that had woven into each other. They pushed the dried leaves aside with their hands and piled up fresh leaves to make headrests on the ground. One of the men made a broom from the branches of a tree, which he used to effectively push the leaves aside. I jumped over the gutter, sat against a tree, and, throughout the night, thought about my uncle and then my father, mother, brothers, friends. Why does everyone keep dying except me? I walked up and down the road trying not to be angry.

In the morning people stood up and dusted themselves off with their hands. Some of the men washed with dew. They shook leaves of little plants and trees, rubbing the residue of water onto their faces and heads. After hours of waiting impatiently, we heard the clunking of an engine down the road. We weren't sure if it was the bus, so we gathered our bags and hid in the bushes near the road. The sound of the whining engine grew until the bus could finally be seen. Everyone ran out of hiding and hailed the bus until it came to a stop. We hurriedly piled on and were off. As the bus proceeded, the apprentice came around to collect the fare. I paid half price, because I was under eighteen, but half price in those times was more than full price when everything was peaceful. I looked out the window and watched the trees go by. And then the bus began to slow down and the trees were replaced by soldiers with big guns, all aiming at the road, at the bus. They asked everyone to step out of the bus; then they made us walk through a barricade. I looked around, and in the bushes I saw there were more men with submachine guns and grenade launchers. I was observing the formation they had and almost ran into a soldier who was making his way to the bus. He looked at me with bloodshot eyes and a face that said, "I will kill you if I want to and nothing will come of it." The look was familiar to me.

They checked the bus for reasons nobody understood. After a few minutes, everyone was on board again. As we gradually started moving, I watched the barricade disappear and I recalled when we used to attack such barricades. I dismissed the thoughts before I was transported back to those times. There were too many barricades, and at every one of them the soldiers behaved differently. Some demanded money even when passengers had the correct documents. Refusing to pay, one risked being sent back to the city. Those who didn't have money had their watches or jewelry or anything of value taken from them. Whenever we were approaching a roadblock, I would quietly start reciting prayers that I hoped would aid my passing through it.

At about four in the afternoon, the bus reached a town called Kambia, its final destination. For the first time since we left the city, I saw some of the passengers' faces relax a bit. But soon enough, our faces tensed again, and we all grumbled as the immigration officers also asked us to pay before we could cross the boundary. Everyone reached into their socks, the hems of pants, under headties, to get the remainder of their money. A woman with two seven-year-old boys pleaded with the officer, telling him that she needed the money to feed her boys in Conakry. The man just kept his hand out and yelled at the woman to step aside. It sickened me to see that Sierra Leoneans asked money from those who had come from the war. They were benefiting from people who were running for their lives. Why does one have to pay to leave his own country? I thought, but I couldn't argue. I had to pay the money. The immigration officers were asking for three hundred leones, almost two months' pay, to put a departure stamp in passports. As soon as my passport was stamped, I crossed the border into Guinea. I had a long way, over fifty miles, to get to Conakry, the capital, so I walked fast to take another bus that would get me there. I hadn't thought about the fact that I didn't know how to speak any of the languages in Guinea. I became worried a bit but I was relieved to have made it out of my country alive.

The buses to Conakry waited on the other side of a checkpoint that had been erected by Guinean soldiers. There were men standing near the checkpoint selling Guinean currency at whatever rate they pleased. I thought the soldiers would be against such black-market foreign exchange, but they didn't seem to care. I changed my money and walked toward the checkpoint. The border was crowded with soldiers who either didn't speak English or pretended not to. They had their guns in ready positions, as if they expected something to happen. I avoided eye contact, afraid that they might see in my eyes that I had once been a soldier in the war that I was now leaving behind.

There was a dark brown wooden house through which I had to pass to get to the bus. Inside this house the soldiers searched people's bags, and the people would then go outside and present their documents to the officers. When I was in the wooden house, the soldiers tore open my bag and threw all its contents on the floor. I didn't have much, so I had little difficulty repacking: two shirts, two undershirts, and three pairs of pants.

I emerged from the wooden house and felt as if all the soldiers were looking at me. We were to present our documents, but to whom? There were too many tables. I didn't know which one to go to. The soldiers sat under the shade of mango trees dressed in full combat gear. Some had their guns hanging by the straps on their chairs, and others placed theirs on the table, the muzzle facing the wooden house. This way, they made people nervous before they asked them for money.

A soldier who sat on the far right of the lined tables, a cigar in his mouth, motioned for me to come over. He put his hand out for my passport. I gave it to him without looking at his face. The soldier spoke a language that I couldn't understand. He put my passport in his chest pocket, took the cigar out of his mouth, placed his hands on the table, and sternly looked at me. I looked down, but the soldier lifted my chin. He took the cigar out of his mouth and examined my passport again. His eyes were red, but he had a grin on his face. He folded his hands and sat back in his chair, looking at me. I smiled a bit and the soldier laughed at me. He said something in his language and put his hand out on the table again. This time the grin on his face had disappeared. I placed some money in his hands. He smelled the money and put it in his pocket. He pulled my passport out of his pocket and motioned for me to go through the gate.

On the other side were a lot of buses. I was confused about which one to take to Conakry. Everyone I tried to ask for directions didn't understand what I was saying. The only word I knew in French was *bonjour*, which did me no good.

I was confusedly looking for a bus to the capital when I bumped into a passerby.

"Watch wussai you dae go," the passerby grumbled in Krio.

"Me na sorry, sir," I replied. "How de body," I continued, shaking hands with the stranger.

"Me body fine en waitin you dae do na ya so me pekin?" the man asked me.

I told him that I was looking for the right bus to Conakry. He told me that he was heading there as well. The bus was overcrowded, so I stood for most of the trip. In over fifty miles to the capital there were more than fifteen checkpoints and the soldiers were unmerciful. All of the roadblocks looked the same. Jeeps with mounted guns were parked along the road. Two soldiers stood by the metal pole stretched across the road from one gutter to another. On the right, more soldiers sat under a shack covered with tarp. There were a few compartments of the shack, where the soldiers searched people. They had set a fixed price for all Sierra Leoneans; those who couldn't pay were kicked off the bus. I wondered if they sent the people back to the other side of the border. Under the auspices of the man I had boarded the bus with, I was able to pass some of the roadblocks for free. Most of the soldiers thought I was the man's son, so they checked his documents and not mine and charged him for both of us. I don't think he noticed; he just wanted to get to Conakry, and it seemed money wasn't a problem for him. At one of the roadblocks the soldiers took me into a room and made me undress. At first I didn't want to take off my clothes, but I saw them kick a man to the floor and rip his shirt and pants. One of the soldiers took my belt. The belt buckle had the head of a lion on it and it was my favorite. I held my pants with one hand and ran back to the bus. I pressed my teeth hard together and folded my fist, holding back my anger.

At the last roadblock a soldier asked me to put my hands on my head so that he could search me. When I raised my hands, my pants fell down and some of the passengers laughed. The soldier picked up my pants and tied them with a shoelace that he had in his pocket. After he was done, he put his hands in my pocket and took out my passport. He flipped the pages and gave it back to me. I followed behind the people who waited in line to get their entry stamps. I was shaking with anger, but I knew I had to calm myself down if I wanted to make it into Conakry. I overheard people saying that the cost of the entry fee was the equivalent of three hundred leones. I had only a hundred leones and needed it for the rest of my journey. What am I going to do? I thought. I had come all this way for nothing. I couldn't even afford to return to Freetown if I wanted to. Tears had begun to form in my eyes. I was nervous and couldn't see a way out of this. I was beginning to feel anxious when a man whose passport had just been stamped accidentally dropped two of the many bags he carried as he was going around the checkpoint to reboard the bus. I hesitated for a bit but decided to take the chance. I left the line and picked up his bags, following him to the bus. I sat in the backseat, slouching in my seat, and peeked to see if the soldiers were looking in my direction. I sat on the bus until everyone had reboarded it; the soldiers didn't come looking for me. The bus began to pull away slowly and then gathered speed. I had entered the country illegally, which I knew would later become a problem.

As the bus headed for Conakry, I began to worry, since I didn't actually know what to do once I got there. I had heard that the Sierra Leonean ambassador let refugees sleep temporarily in the compound of the embassy, but I had no idea where the embassy itself was located. I was sitting next to a Fulani fellow by the name of Jalloh, who said he had lived in Freetown. We talked about what the war had done to the country. Afterward, he gave me his phone number and asked me to call him if I needed help getting around the city. I wanted to tell him that I had no place to stay, but he got off before I could summon the nerve to confide in him. I looked about the bus for the Sierra Leonean man I had bumped into but I couldn't find him. A few minutes later, the bus came to a halt at a huge station, its final destination. I got out and watched everyone go. I sighed and placed my hands on my head, then walked to a bench and sat down. I covered my face with my hands. "I can't sit here all night," I kept mumbling to myself.

There were lots of taxis, and all the people who arrived at the bus station took them. I didn't want to stand out as a lost foreigner, so I took a taxi, too. The driver said something in French. I knew that he was asking where I wanted to go. "Sierra Leone consulate, ahh, embassy," I told the driver. I looked out the window at the utility poles and the sloppily hung streetlights; their lights seemed brighter than the moonlight. The taxi stopped in front of the embassy and the driver pointed to the green, white, and blue flag to make sure that I was at the right place. I nodded and paid him. When I got out, the guards at the embassy door, speaking Krio, asked me for my passport. I showed it to them and they let me into the compound.

Inside were more than fifty people, probably in the same situation as I. Most were lying on mats in the open compound. Their bundles or bags stood next to them. Others were removing their mats from their luggage. I assumed people only slept here at night and went out during the daytime. I found a spot in the corner, sat on the ground, and leaned against the wall, breathing heavily. The sight of all these people reminded me of a few villages I had passed through while running away from the war. I was scared and worried about what turmoil the next day might bring. Nonetheless, I was happy to have made it out of Freetown, to have escaped the possibility of becoming a soldier again. This gave me some comfort. I took out the remaining raw rice from my bag and started chewing on it. There was a woman sitting with her two children, a boy and a girl no more than seven years old, a few paces from me. She was whispering a story to them, as she didn't want to disturb other people. As I watched the elaborate movements of her hands, the tide of my thoughts took me to a particular telling of a story I had heard many times as a boy.

It was nighttime and we sat by the fire stretching our arms toward the flames as we listened to stories and watched the moon and the stars retire. The red coal from the firewood lit our faces in the dark and wisps of smoke continuously rose toward the sky. *Pa* Sesay, one of my friends' grandfather, had told us many stories that night, but before he began telling the last story, he repeatedly said, "This is a very important story." He then cleared his throat and began:

"There was a hunter who went into the bush to kill a monkey. He had looked for only a few minutes when he saw a monkey sitting comfortably in the branch of a low tree. The monkey didn't pay him any attention, not even when his footsteps on the dried leaves rose and fell as he neared. When he was close enough and behind a tree where he could clearly see the monkey, he raised his rifle and aimed. Just when he was about to pull the trigger, the monkey spoke: 'If you shoot me, your mother will die, and if you don't, your father will die.' The monkey resumed its position, chewing its food, and every so often scratched its head or the side of its belly.

"What would you do if you were the hunter?"

This was a story told to young people in my village once a year. The storyteller, usually an elder, would pose this unanswerable question at the end of the story in the presence of the children's parents. Every child who was present at the gathering was asked to give an answer, but no child ever did, since their mother and father were both present. The storyteller never offered an answer either. During each of these gatherings, when it was my time to respond, I always told the storyteller that I would think it over, which of course was not a good enough answer.

After such gatherings, my peers and I—all the children between the ages of six and twelve—would brainstorm several possible answers that would avoid the death of one of our parents. There was no right answer. If you spared the monkey, someone was going to die, and if you didn't, someone would also die.

That night we agreed on an answer, but it was immediately rejected. We told *Pa* Sesay that if any of us was the hunter, we wouldn't have gone hunting for monkeys. We told him, "There are other animals such as deer to hunt."

"That is not an acceptable answer," he said. "We are assuming that you as the hunter had already raised your gun and have to make the decision." He broke his kola nut in half and smiled before putting a piece in his mouth.

When I was seven I had an answer to this question that made sense to me. I never discussed it with anyone, though, for fear of how my mother would feel. I concluded to myself that if I were the hunter, I would shoot the monkey so that it would no longer have the chance to put other hunters in the same predicament.

CHRONOLOGY

It is believed, though not recorded in written form, that the Bullom (Sherbro) people were present along the coast of Sierra Leone before the 1200s, if not earlier—before European contact with Sierra Leone. By the beginning of the 1400s, many tribes from other parts of Africa had migrated and settled in what came to be known as Sierra Leone. Among these tribes were the Temne. They settled along the northern coast of present-day Sierra Leone, and the Mende, another major tribe, occupied the south. There were fifteen additional tribes scattered in different parts of the country.

1462   The written history of Sierra Leone begins when Portuguese explorers land, naming the mountains surrounding what is now Freetown Serra Lyoa (Lion Mountains) due to their leonine shape.

1500–early 1700s   European traders stop regularly on the Sierra Leone Peninsula, exchanging cloth and metal goods for ivory, timber, and a small number of slaves.

1652   The first slaves in North America are brought from Sierra Leone to the Sea Islands, off the coast of the southern United States.

1700–1800   A slave trade thrives between Sierra Leone and the plantations of South Carolina and Georgia, where the slaves' rice-farming skills make them particularly valuable.

1787   British abolitionists help four hundred freed slaves from the United States, Nova Scotia, and Britain return to Africa to settle in what they call the "Province of Freedom," in Sierra Leone. These Krio, as they come to be called, are from all areas of Africa.

1791   Other groups of freed slaves join the "Province of Freedom" settlement, and it soon becomes known as Freetown, the name of the current capital of Sierra Leone.

1792   Freetown becomes one of Britain's first colonies in West Africa.

1800   Freed slaves from Jamaica arrive in Freetown.

1808   Sierra Leone becomes a British crown colony. The British government uses Freetown as its naval base for antislavery patrols.

1821–1874   Freetown serves as the residence of the British governor, who also rules the Gold Coast (now Ghana) and Gambia settlements.

1827   Fourah Bay College is established and rapidly becomes a magnet for English-speaking Africans on the West Coast. For more than a century, it is the only European-style university in western sub-Saharan Africa.

1839   Slaves aboard a ship called the *Amistad* revolt to secure their freedom. Their leader, Sengbe Pieh—or Joseph Cinque, as he becomes known in the United States—is a young Mende man from Sierra Leone.

1898   Britain imposes a hut tax in Sierra Leone, decreeing that the inhabitants of the new protectorate be taxed on the size of their huts as payment for the privilege of British administration. This sparks two rebellions in the hinterland: one by the Temne tribe and the other by the Mende tribe.

1951   A constitution is enacted by the British to give some power to the inhabitants, providing a framework for decolonization.

1953   Local ministerial responsibility is introduced, and Sir Milton Margai is appointed chief minister.

1960   Sir Milton Margai becomes prime minister following the completion of successful constitutional talks in London.

April 27, 1961   Sierra Leone becomes independent, with Sir Milton Margai as its first prime minister. The country opts for a parliamentary system within the Commonwealth of Nations. The following year, Sir Milton Margai's Sierra Leone Peoples Party (SLPP), which led the country to independence, wins the first general election under universal adult franchise.

1964   Sir Milton Margai dies, and his half brother Sir Albert Margai succeeds him as prime minister.

May 1967   In closely contested elections, the All People's Congress (APC) wins a plurality of the parliamentary seats. Accordingly, the governor general (representing the British monarch) declares Siaka Stevens—APC leader and mayor of Freetown—the new prime minister. Within a few hours, Stevens and Albert Margai are placed under house arrest by Brigadier David Lansana, the commander of the Republic of Sierra Leone Military Forces (RSLMF), on grounds that the determination of office should await the election of the tribal representatives to the house. Another group of officers soon stages another coup, only to be later ousted in a third coup, the "sergeants' revolt."

1968   With a return to civilian rule, Siaka Stevens at last assumes office as prime minister. However, tranquility is not completely restored. In November, a state of emergency is declared after provincial disturbances.

1971   The government survives an unsuccessful military coup. Also, a republican constitution is adopted, and Siaka Stevens becomes the first president of the republic.

1974   Another failed military coup is launched against the government.

1977   Students demonstrate against government corruption and embezzlement of funds.

1978   The constitution is amended, and all political parties, other than the ruling APC, are banned. Sierra Leone becomes a one-party state, with the APC as its sole legal party.

1985   Siaka Stevens retires and appoints Major General Joseph Saidu Momoh the next president of Sierra Leone. Momoh's APC rule is marked by increasing abuses of power.

March 1991   A small band of men who call themselves the Revolutionary United Front (RUF), under the leadership of a former corporal, Foday Sankoh, begin to attack villages in eastern Sierra Leone, on the Liberian border. The initial group is made up of Charles Taylor's rebels and a few mercenaries from Burkina Faso. Their goal is to rid the country of the corrupt APC government. Fighting continues in the ensuing months, with the RUF gaining control of the diamond mines in the Kono district and pushing the Sierra Leone army back toward Freetown.

April 1992   A group of young military officers, led by Captain Valentine Strasser, launches a military coup that sends Momoh into exile. They establish the National Provisional Ruling Council (NPRC) as the ruling authority in Sierra Leone. The NPRC proves to be nearly as ineffectual as the Momoh government at repelling the RUF. More and more of the country falls into the hands of the RUF fighters.

1995   The RUF holds much of the countryside and are on the doorstep of Freetown. To control the situation, the NPRC hires several hundred mercenaries from private firms. Within a month, they have driven the RUF fighters back to enclaves along Sierra Leone's borders.

1996   Valentine Strasser is ousted and replaced by Brigadier General Julius Maada Bio, his defense minister. As a result of popular demand and mounting international pressure, the NPRC, under Maada Bio, agrees to hand over power to a civilian government via presidential and parliamentary elections, which are held in March 1996. Ahmad Tejan Kabbah, a diplomat who worked at the UN for more than twenty years, wins the presidential election under the banner of the SLPP.

May 1997   Kabbah is overthrown by the Armed Forces Revolutionary Council (AFRC), a military junta headed by Lieutenant Colonel Johnny Paul Koroma, and the junta invites the RUF to participate in the new government.

March 1998   The AFRC is ousted by the Nigerian-led ECOWAS Monitoring Group (ECOMOG) forces, and the democratically elected government of President Kabbah is reinstated.

January 1999   The RUF launches another attempt to overthrow the government. Fighting reaches parts of Freetown again, leaving thousands dead and wounded. ECOMOG forces drive back the RUF attack several weeks later.

July 1999   The Lomé Peace Accord is signed between President Kabbah and Foday Sankoh of the RUF. The agreement grants the rebels seats in a new government and all forces a general amnesty from prosecution. The government has largely ceased to function effectively, however, and at least half of its territory remains under rebel control. In October, the UN Security Council establishes the United Nations Mission in Sierra Leone (UNAMSIL) to help implement the peace agreement.

April/May 2000   Violence and rebel activity return, most notably when RUF forces hold hundreds of UNAMSIL personnel hostage, taking possession of their arms and ammunition. In May, members of the RUF shoot and kill as many as twenty people demonstrating outside Sankoh's house in Freetown against RUF violations. As a result of these events, which violate the peace agreement, Sankoh and other senior members of the RUF are arrested, and the group is stripped of its position in the government. In early May, a new cease-fire agreement is signed in Abuja. However, disarmament, demobilization, and reintegration (DDR) does not resume, and fighting continues.

May 2000   The situation in the country has deteriorated to such an extent that British troops are deployed in Operation Palliser to evacuate foreign nationals. They stabilize the situation and are the catalyst for a cease-fire and the end of the civil war.

2001   A second Abuja Peace Agreement is signed to set the stage for a resumption of DDR on a wide scale. This brings about a significant reduction in hostilities. As disarmament progresses, the government begins to reassert its authority in formerly rebel-held areas.

January 2002   President Kabbah declares the civil war officially over.

May 2002   President Kabbah and his party, the SLPP, win landslide victories in the presidential and legislative elections. Kabbah is reelected for a five-year term.

July 28, 2002   The British withdraw a 200-man military contingent that had been in the country since the summer of 2000, leaving behind a 105-man-strong team to train the Sierra Leone army.

Summer 2002   Both the Truth and Reconciliation Commission (TRC) and the Special Court begin to function. The Lomé Accord calls for the establishment of a Truth and Reconciliation Commission to provide a forum for both victims and perpetrators of human rights violations to tell their stories, and to facilitate genuine reconciliation. Subsequently, the Sierra Leonean government asks the UN to help set up a Special Court for Sierra Leone, which will try those who "bear the greatest responsibility for the commission of crimes against humanity, war crimes and serious violations of international humanitarian law, as well as crimes under relevant Sierra Leonean law within the territory of Sierra Leone since November 30, 1996."

November 2002   UNAMSIL begins a gradual reduction in personnel, from a peak level of 17,500.

October 2004   The Truth and Reconciliation Commission releases its final report to the government, although widespread public distribution is delayed until August 2005 because of editing and printing problems. The government releases a white paper in June 2005, accepting some and rejecting or ignoring a number of other recommendations. Civil society groups dismiss the response as too vague and continue to criticize the government for its failure to follow up on the report's recommendations.

December 2005   The UNAMSIL peacekeeping mission formally ends, and the UN Integrated Office in Sierra Leone (UNIOSIL) is established, assuming a peace-building mandate.

March 25, 2006   After discussions with the newly elected Liberian president, Ellen Johnson-Sirleaf, President Olusegun Obasanjo of Nigeria says that Liberia is free to take Charles Taylor, who has been living in exile in Nigeria, into custody. Two days later, Taylor attempts to flee Nigeria, but is apprehended and transferred to Freetown under UN guard by nightfall on March 29. He is currently incarcerated in a UN jail, awaiting trial at the Special Court for Sierra Leone (SCSL) on eleven counts of war crimes.

ACKNOWLEDGMENTS

I never thought that I would be alive to this day, much less that I would write a book. During this second lifetime of mine, a lot of remarkable individuals have given meaning to my life, opened their hearts and doors to me, supported and believed in me and all my undertakings. Without their presence, this book wouldn't have been possible. My immense gratitude to my family: my mother, Laura Simms, for her tireless work to bring me here, for her love and advice, for providing me a home when I had none, and for allowing me to rest and enjoy the last moments of what was left of my childhood; my aunts, Heather Greer, Fran Silverberg, and Shantha Bloemen, for your good listening, kind hearts, generosity, love, emotional support, all the meaningful moments, and everything; my sister, Erica Henegen, for your trust, honesty, and love, and for all those insightful long nights we spent grappling with the reasons for our existence; and Bernard Matambo, my brother, for your friendship and intelligence, for our common dreams and unremitting strength to carry on and enjoy every moment of our lives, and for making all those long nights at the library meaningful and unforgettable. Thanks, Chale. My cousin Aminata and my childhood friend Mohamed, I am so very happy to have you back in my life and indebted to you for bringing those happy memories of a past that you and I share.

I am indebted to Marge Scheuer and the entire Scheuer family for your ceaseless financial support, which enabled me to complete my studies and accomplish things beyond my dreams. Thank you so much. My gratitude to everyone at the Blue Ridge and Four Oaks Foundations, to Joseph Cotton and Tracey for looking after me as your little brother and setting me straight, to Mary Sobel for checking in and making sure all is well, and to Lisa, for everything.

I am very grateful to a lot of professors at Oberlin College. Professor Laurie McMillin gave me the confidence I needed to start writing seriously. I am indebted to Professor Dan Chaon for his patience, tutelage, confidence, honesty, friendship, and support in making this book a reality. Thank you, Dan, you taught me well and made sure that I completed this book. My gratitude to Professor Sylvia Watanabe, for all your support, friendship, and good counsel, and for your unceasing quest to enrich my creative life; and to Professors Yakubu Saaka and Ben Schiff, for your good advice, always.

My dear friends Paul Fogel and Yvette Chalom: thank you for your unceasing care for my well-being, for your advice, for opening your house to me during the writing of this book, and for being two of my early readers—your comments helped tremendously to shape this work. I am very grateful for everything. Thank you, Priscilla Hayner, Jo Becker, and Pam Bruns, for your encouragement, friendship, and insights on the earlier drafts.

I am very lucky to have Ira Silverberg as my agent. Thank you for all your insightful advice, your friendship, and your patience with explaining the workings of the publishing world. Without you I would have gotten easily frustrated. My editor, Sarah Crichton, thank you so very much for all your hard work. I am grateful for your honesty, your careful and compassionate treatment of this deeply personal and emotionally charged material, and all the gossip before and after each meeting that helped to lighten things. I love working with you and I learned so much from this process. Thank you to Rose Lichter-Marck for following up and making sure I didn't procrastinate, and my gratitude to everyone at Farrar, Straus and Giroux for all your hard work and friendship.

My friends Melvin Jimenez, Matt Moore, Lauren Hyman, and Marielle Ramsay, thanks for your friendship, for keeping in touch, and for understand-

ing that I needed time away from everyone to complete this work. To everyone
who has opened their hearts or doors to me, thank you so very much.

Last, I am very grateful to Danièle Fogel for all your emotional support:
your love, patience, and understanding during the writing of this book. Without your friendship and care, it would have been more difficult to embark on
this journey, especially while at Oberlin College.